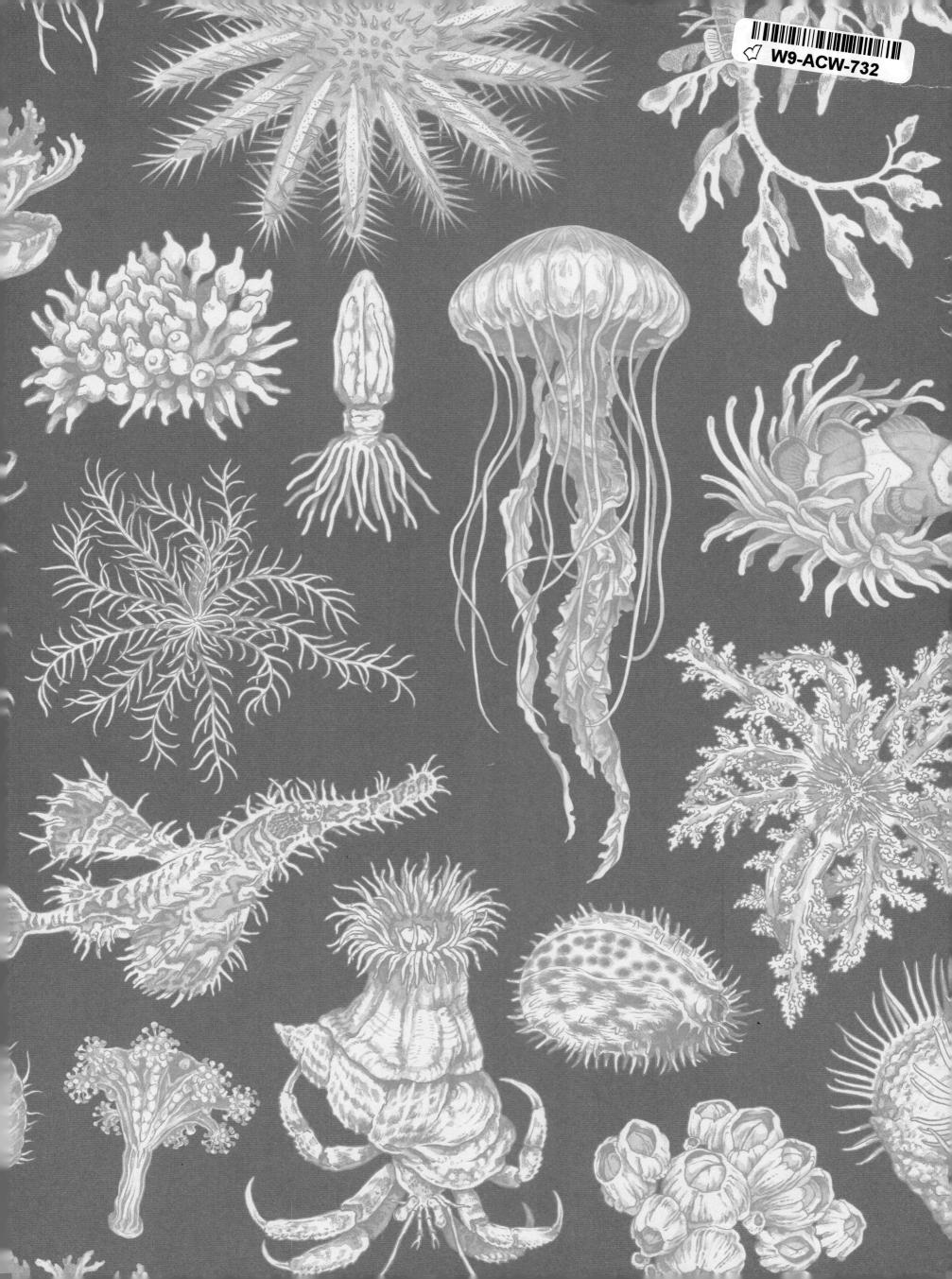

Oceanarium

For all my friends at the NMA and for Isabella and Charlie,
future ocean optimists
LT

For Arcadia Beach
TW

First US edition 2022
First published by Big Picture Press, an imprint of Bonnier Books UK, 2021

Library of Congress Catalog Card Number 2021946700
ISBN 978-1-5362-2381-1

21 22 23 24 25 26 WKT 10 9 8 7 6 5 4 3 2 1

Printed in Shenzhen, Guangdong, China

This book was typeset in Gill Sans, Mrs Green, and Modern20 BT.
The illustrations were done in graphite and watercolor with color added digitally.

BIG PICTURE PRESS
an imprint of
Candlewick Press
99 Dover Street
Somerville, Massachusetts 02144

www.candlewick.com

Welcome to the Museum · ADMIT ALL

Oceanarium

illustrated by TEAGAN WHITE

written by LOVEDAY TRINICK

BPP

Preface

Viewed from space, Earth's surface is dominated by water, a vast area of blue. This makes our planet different from every other in the solar system, and potentially unique in our universe. It is because we have water that life can exist.

The ocean supports all life, both underwater and on land. It affects our climate, dictates our weather patterns, and provides half the oxygen we breathe. Yet despite the ocean's importance, humans have only explored a tiny portion of it, and new discoveries are made every time we venture into the deep.

Many scientists believe that life on earth began in the ocean, overcoming cataclysmic asteroid strikes and toxic conditions to later emerge on land. From these microbial life-forms evolved every type of creature we see aboveground today. Living things continued to evolve underwater, too, responding to changes in their environment and creating an explosion of diversity, capable of thriving in every type of habitat. Today, we know of around 230,000 species of animals and plants living in the ocean, but it is thought that there could be as many as two million yet to be discovered.

As fast as we are finding new life, however, we could also be losing it. With climate change and pollution caused by humans driving this loss, it is more important than ever to learn about, explore, enjoy, and protect the ocean, not only for the life we find there but also for our future generations. It is only when we begin to understand the wonder of this wild habitat that we can appreciate its role in our lives.

Loveday Trinick
The National Marine Aquarium, Plymouth, United Kingdom

Entrance

Welcome to Oceanarium

This is no ordinary aquarium. Open twenty-four hours a day, seven days a week, each exhibit showcases the ocean's inhabitants as you have never seen them before. See the world's largest animal, inspect some of the smallest creatures, and marvel at the kaleidoscope of colors, shapes, and sizes of life underwater.

Stroll through this book to tour the aquarium, and discover the majesty that the ocean holds. From the sunlit shallows to the darkest depths, in the pages that follow you will find extraordinary creatures that normally lie hidden beneath the waves.

Take a moment to inspect each habitat carefully. You will be amazed at what you find. There are some species who are nearly as old as life itself, slowly patrolling the open waters in search of their next meal. There are others whose scales glint and shimmer as they dart nervously among coral. Some are so perfectly still on the seabed that you may not notice them at all. And others are magicians, changing color and form to seemingly disappear in plain sight.

Pass through the aquarium's halls and learn about our precious connection with the ocean, and how its future may well hold the key to our own future. By learning how the ocean and humanity interact, we can begin to better understand our complex relationship with the ocean and overcome the challenges we currently face.

Enter *Oceanarium* and discover the secrets of the sea for yourself. From the majestic to the peculiar, the fearsome to the vulnerable, this awe-inspiring world is laid before you to explore.

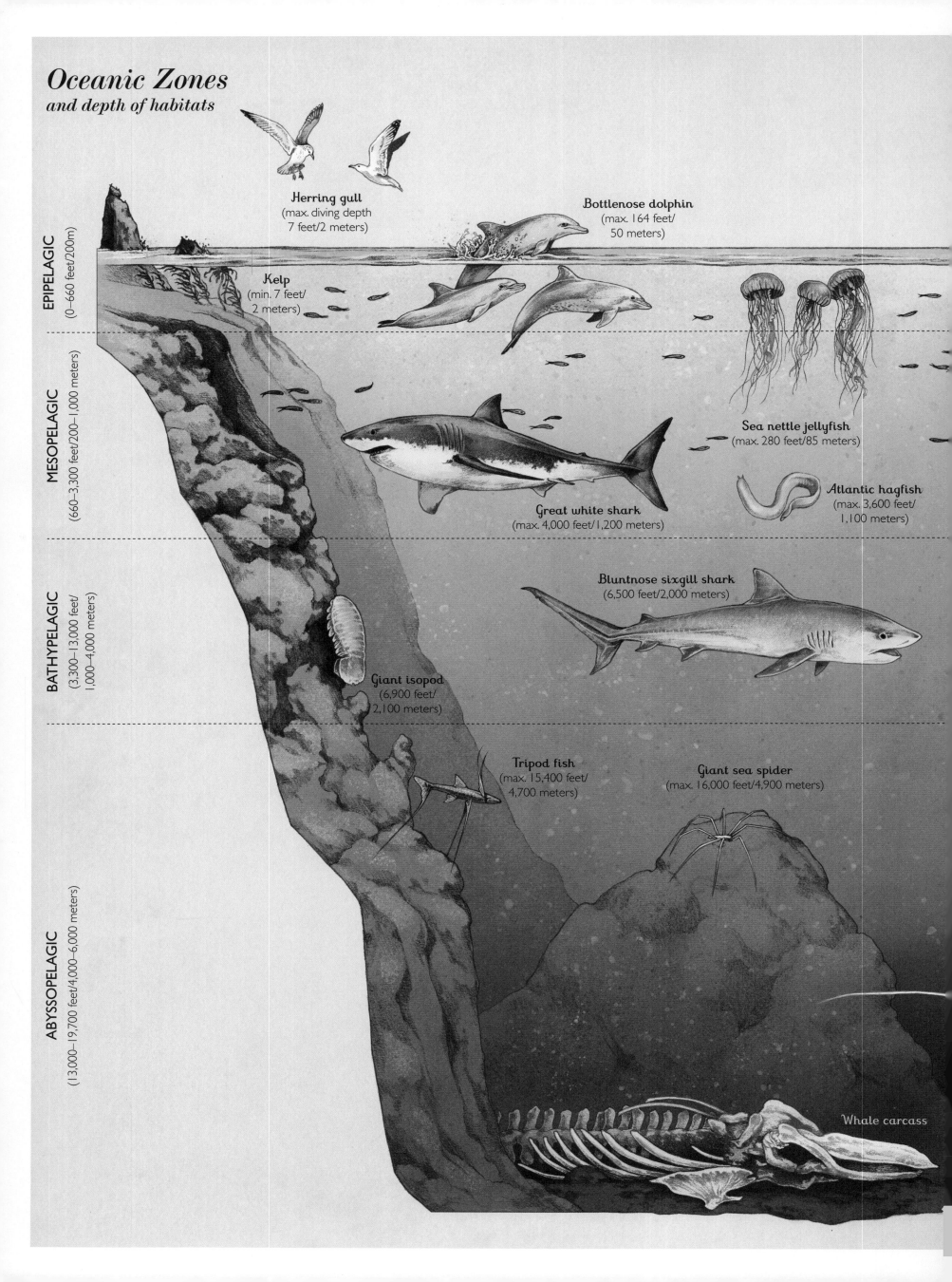

Oceanic Zones
and depth of habitats

EPIPELAGIC (0–660 feet/200m)

MESOPELAGIC (660–3,300 feet/200–1,000 meters)

BATHYPELAGIC (3,300–13,000 feet/1,000–4,000 meters)

ABYSSOPELAGIC (13,000–19,700 feet/4,000–6,000 meters)

Herring gull
(max. diving depth
7 feet/2 meters)

Bottlenose dolphin
(max. 164 feet/
50 meters)

Kelp
(min. 7 feet/
2 meters)

Sea nettle jellyfish
(max. 280 feet/85 meters)

Great white shark
(max. 4,000 feet/1,200 meters)

Atlantic hagfish
(max. 3,600 feet/
1,100 meters)

Bluntnose sixgill shark
(6,500 feet/2,000 meters)

Giant isopod
(6,900 feet/
2,100 meters)

Tripod fish
(max. 15,400 feet/
4,700 meters)

Giant sea spider
(max. 16,000 feet/4,900 meters)

Whale carcass

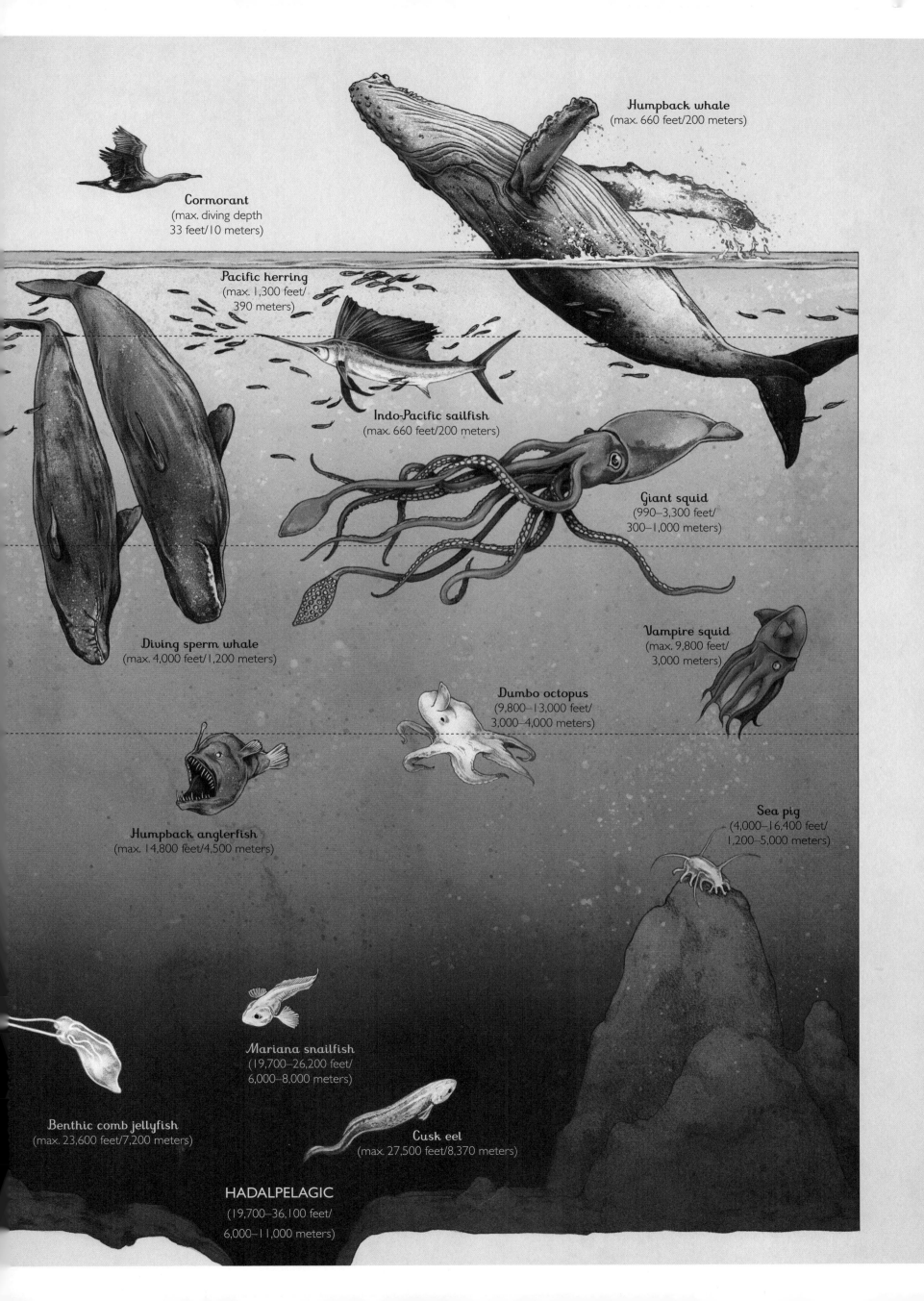

Humpback whale
(max. 660 feet/200 meters)

Cormorant
(max. diving depth
33 feet/10 meters)

Pacific herring
(max. 1,300 feet/
390 meters)

Indo-Pacific sailfish
(max. 660 feet/200 meters)

Giant squid
(990–3,300 feet/
300–1,000 meters)

Diving sperm whale
(max. 4,000 feet/1,200 meters)

Vampire squid
(max. 9,800 feet/
3,000 meters)

Dumbo octopus
(9,800–13,000 feet/
3,000–4,000 meters)

Sea pig
(4,000–16,400 feet/
1,200–5,000 meters)

Humpback anglerfish
(max. 14,800 feet/4,500 meters)

Mariana snailfish
(19,700–26,200 feet/
6,000–8,000 meters)

Benthic comb jellyfish
(max. 23,600 feet/7,200 meters)

Cusk eel
(max. 27,500 feet/8,370 meters)

HADALPELAGIC

(19,700–36,100 feet/
6,000–11,000 meters)

ENTRANCE

Ocean Zones

When we look out to sea, we are seeing only a tiny portion of what is the most significant feature of our planet. The ocean is millions of times larger than our view of the horizon, and with an average of nearly 2½ miles/4 kilometers of water below the surface, diving beneath the waves reveals a world unseen by most people.

The ocean is the largest habitat on earth and its scale is difficult to imagine—the tallest feature on land, Mount Everest, could fit inside the 36,000-foot-/11,000-meter-deep Mariana Trench with 6,500 feet/2,000 meters to spare. Containing 99 percent of all the living space available to animals and plants on our planet, the ocean changes as you descend through the watery depths, leading to the evolution of some of the most incredible species.

As you plunge from the ocean's surface, sunlight decreases. The faint light that can be seen at around 330 feet/100 meters disappears entirely at 660 feet/200 meters. Seaweeds and other photosynthetic life thrive in the illuminated upper level, supporting a variety of creatures including most marine mammals, sea turtles, and fish.

When you venture into the darkness, the pressure begins to intensify. Dive to 3,300 feet/1,000 meters (the depth at which sperm whales are known to hunt) and the pressure is one hundred times greater than on the water's surface—enough to crush most living things that live in shallower water. Even in this most extreme of environments, the flickering glow of bioluminescent species can still be seen, and unique scuttling crabs and graceful jellies swarm around smoking hydrothermal vents. These vents are fissures in the ocean floor above red-hot magma, which warms the water and provides a hospitable environment for bacteria that are an important food source for deep-sea animals.

At the deepest zone—the hadalpelagic trenches—the pressure is an incredible 9 tons/8 metric tons per square inch and temperatures struggle to rise above freezing. It was once thought that no life could possibly exist here, but the early explorers Don Walsh and Jacques Piccard disproved this idea when they descended into the Mariana Trench—an almost impossible five-hour journey. In this inhospitable environment, giant insect-like creatures can be found scavenging for food fallen from the surface 7 miles/11 kilometers away.

Blue Planet

The history of Earth's ocean starts with the beginnings of the universe. This story takes us back 13.8 billion years to the Big Bang, when vast amounts of hydrogen gas formed. Hundreds of millions of years later, when the universe had cooled, oxygen atoms appeared and the first water molecules were created. Those same water molecules that originated from the universe's tumultuous beginnings are still in existence today. They have floated in our rivers and lakes, passed through living beings from dinosaurs to humans and trees to plants, and traveled from high in the atmosphere to deep underground.

While many planets and moons have been found to have water in the form of gas or ice, few possess it as a liquid. This is what makes our planet special. Earth is the ideal distance from the sun for water to exist—any closer and temperatures would be too hot, causing water to evaporate, any farther away and it would be too cold, causing water to freeze. With a protective atmosphere kept in place by a strong magnetic field, this precious liquid is safeguarded from being lost to space. Water is what enables all life-forms to flourish.

There may have been a time when water didn't exist on our planet at all. Some scientists believe that most of it arrived as the universe was forming and asteroids and meteorites containing water crashed onto Earth from space. There is also evidence that water in the form of vapor was present in the very early days of our planet and, as Earth cooled, it condensed and fell as rain. Centuries of rainfall may have filled enormous craters on our planet, and they remain full to this day in the form of oceans.

The ocean has changed shape since those early days. The land was once connected as one giant supercontinent known as Pangaea; similarly the ocean would have existed as one enormous basin. In the unimaginably long stretches of geological time since, landmasses have broken apart as the planet's crust collides and shifts. The ocean also moved but remains connected. Today, it is possible to travel around our whole planet without touching land once—a journey of about 20,000 miles/32,000 kilometers.

We have come a long way since our planet formed. Our ocean today is estimated to contain around 3.1 million cubic miles/1.3 billion cubic kilometers of water and is teeming with life. It is the most defining hallmark of our planet, covering more than 70 percent of Earth's surface. From space, it is clear just how much this incredible feature characterizes our home, prompting Earth's colorful epithet: the Blue Planet.

Key to plate

1: **Spilhaus divides**
In 1942, Dr. Athelstan F. Spilhaus created a map to show the ocean as one continuous body of water. This series of globes shows where Spilhaus interrupted the land to depict the ocean as a whole.

2: **Spilhaus projection with ocean currents**
Unlike a traditional world map, Spilhaus's maps focus on Earth's water distribution and display it as a prominent feature. The currents in the ocean are driven by water at different densities. Cold, salty water is dense and sinks, whereas warm, fresh water is lighter and floats. The arrows on the map show where the deep cold currents (blue) and the warm surface currents (red) are. These currents carry not only water around the planet but also energy, which affects our weather and climate.

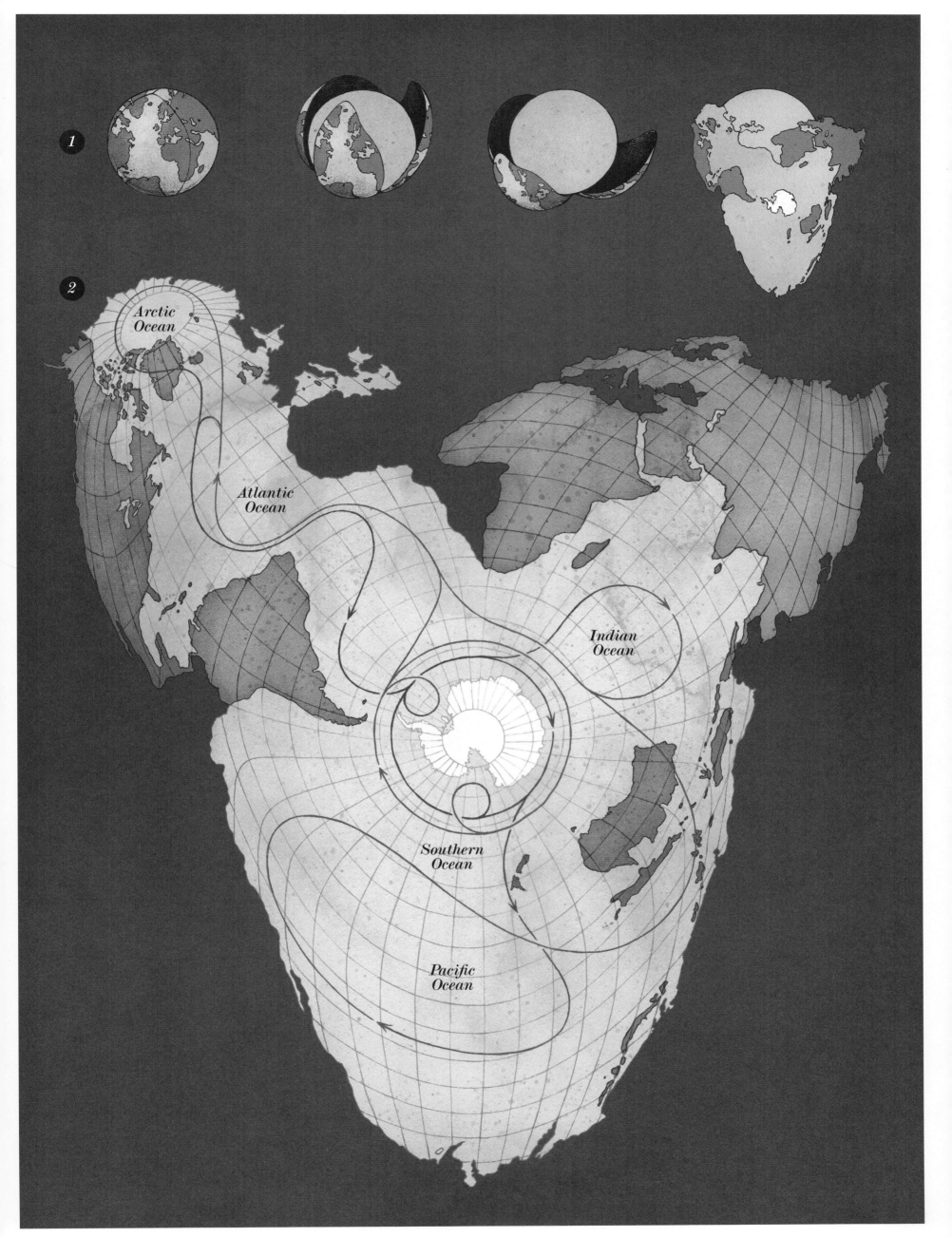

1

2

Arctic
Ocean

Atlantic
Ocean

Indian
Ocean

Southern
Ocean

Pacific
Ocean

Gallery 1

Plankton

Phytoplankton

Zooplankton

Phytoplankton

The ocean is home to some of the smallest and biggest creatures that have ever lived. Among the smallest are plankton—microscopic organisms that drift through the sea as nomads, carried by the ocean currents and unable to swim against them. Plankton are so small that most are measured in micrometers—$^2/5$ inch/1 centimeter is the equivalent of 10,000 micrometers.

Some plankton behave a little like plants and are known as phytoplankton. Just like flora on land, phytoplankton can make their own food via photosynthesis. Oxygen is a by-product of this process, and scientists estimate that around half the oxygen in earth's atmosphere was made by plankton. It is because of photosynthesis that phytoplankton are primary producers, positioned at the bottom of the food chain in the ocean. They are vitally important because they support a whole ecosystem, providing food for many ocean animals, from tiny animal plankton to giant whale sharks.

Because they need sunlight to photosynthesize, phytoplankton must stay near the ocean's surface. With more sunlight encouraging reproduction in the spring and summer months, phytoplankton grow in large numbers during what are known as blooms. These natural occurrences fuel explosions of life in the ocean, but too much phytoplankton can be damaging. Harmful algal blooms are dangerous swellings that can create toxins and deplete oxygen levels, resulting in dead zones where marine animals and plants are unable to survive. This can happen when fertilizer washes off farmland and into the sea, rapidly increasing growth of the algae population. It is a reminder that the ocean is not immune to our activities on land.

Key to plate

1: **Cyanobacteria**
Prochlorococcus marinus
Diameter: Approx. 0.6 micrometers
This minuscule plankton is one of the most abundant photosynthetic organisms on earth. Twenty drops of seawater can contain around 100,000 *P. marinus* cyanobacteria.

2: **Dinoflagellate**
Ceratium ranipes
Diameter: Up to 200 micrometers
During the day, this dinoflagellate extends its "fingers" into the water. These contain chloroplasts that are used in photosynthesis.

3: **Diatom**
Ditylum brightwellii
Length: Up to 300 micrometers
This tiny, single-celled alga has a body made out of glass-like silica—meaning it effectively lives in a greenhouse.

4: **Coccolithophore**
Emiliania huxleyi
Length: Approx. 3.5 micrometers
Coccolithophores have a covering of chalky discs that reflect sunlight. When *E. huxleyi* blooms, this reflection of light is visible to satellites in space.

5: **Sea sparkle**
Noctiluca scintillans
Diameter: Up to 2,000 micrometers
This species makes light via bioluminescence when disturbed, producing an ethereal blue-green glow.

6: **Chaetoceros debilis**
Length: Up to 20 micrometers
These microscopic algae join together to form long, spiral-shaped chains.

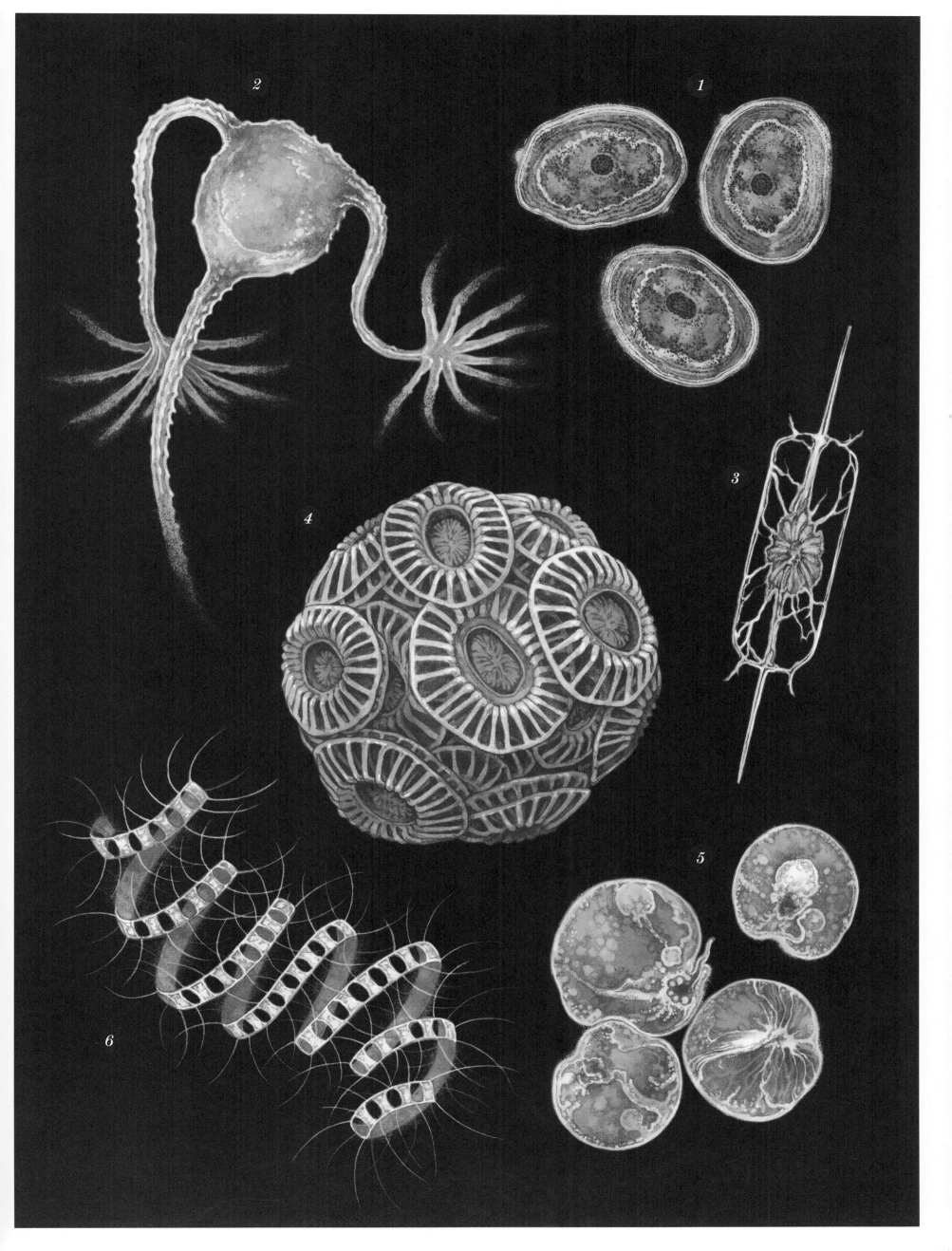

Zooplankton

A group of mainly microscopic creatures, tiny zooplankton drift on the ocean currents. Some of them are the larvae of animals and will grow and eventually mature into crabs, fish, and other recognizable sea creatures; others, such as copepods, will remain minuscule organisms their whole lives. Floating by the thousands in every drop of water on the ocean's surface, they, along with phytoplankton, form a "soup" full of life, which will ultimately feed almost every other animal in the ocean.

Both phytoplankton and zooplankton play an important role in ocean food chains. While phytoplankton use the sun's energy to make food, zooplankton provide the link between phytoplankton and larger sea creatures. Some are herbivorous, grazing directly on phytoplankton, while others are predatory and hunt for smaller zooplankton. Many are eaten by larger animals—blue whales can consume up to 4½ tons/4 metric tons of krill in a single day (see pages 62–63).

Meroplankton are the larvae of animals such as crustaceans and cnidarian that sink from the ocean's surface when they are grown to live in a variety of habitats, from coral reefs to the deep sea. Larvae will often look very different from the adults that they will become—ocean sunfish larvae, for example, are only 2 millimeters in length and are covered with spines, while adults lose their spines and can grow to nearly 6½ feet/2 meters long.

Despite their minute size, zooplankton travel from the ocean's surface to the murky depths and back again every day. This is called vertical migration and it allows them to feed on phytoplankton in the surface waters at night, avoiding predators that cruise there during the day. With trillions of these animals completing a daily round trip of around 6,500 feet/2,000 meters, this is one of the largest migration events on earth.

Key to plate

1: Sea butterfly
Limaicna helicina
Shell width: Up to 6mm
This tiny snail is particularly important to one sea slug called a sea angel, which feeds almost exclusively on it.

2: Polychaete worm
Tomopteris sp.
Length: Up to 2 inches/5 centimeters
Some tomopteris worms make yellow bioluminescence, a rare color in the deep sea.

3: Sea star larvae
Asterias sp.
Length: Approx. 1 millimeter
These larvae eventually get too heavy to float on the ocean's surface and sink to the seabed. At this point, they start to develop into more mature-looking sea stars.

4: Copepod
Calanus glacialis
Length: Up to 5.5 millimeters
There are around 13,000 species of copepod. This species lives in the Arctic and swims between the ocean's surface and up to 5,900 feet/1,800 meters deep.

5: Green crab larvae
Carcinus maenas
Length: Up to 4 millimeters
Animals that inhabit the seafloor, such as this crab, benefit from having planktonic young, as the larvae can drift vast distances before settling.

6: Swordfish larvae
Xiphias gladius
Length: 4 millimeters when newly hatched

As an adult, this highly recognizable predator reaches around 10 feet/3 meters long.

7: Ocean sunfish larvae
Mola mola
Length: Approx. 2 millimeters
The difference in size between the larvae and the adult is one of the biggest known, meaning they grow more than any other animal on earth.

8: Antarctic krill
Euphausia superba
Length: Up to 2 inches/6 centimeters
By weight, these little crustaceans are likely to be the most abundant animals on earth.

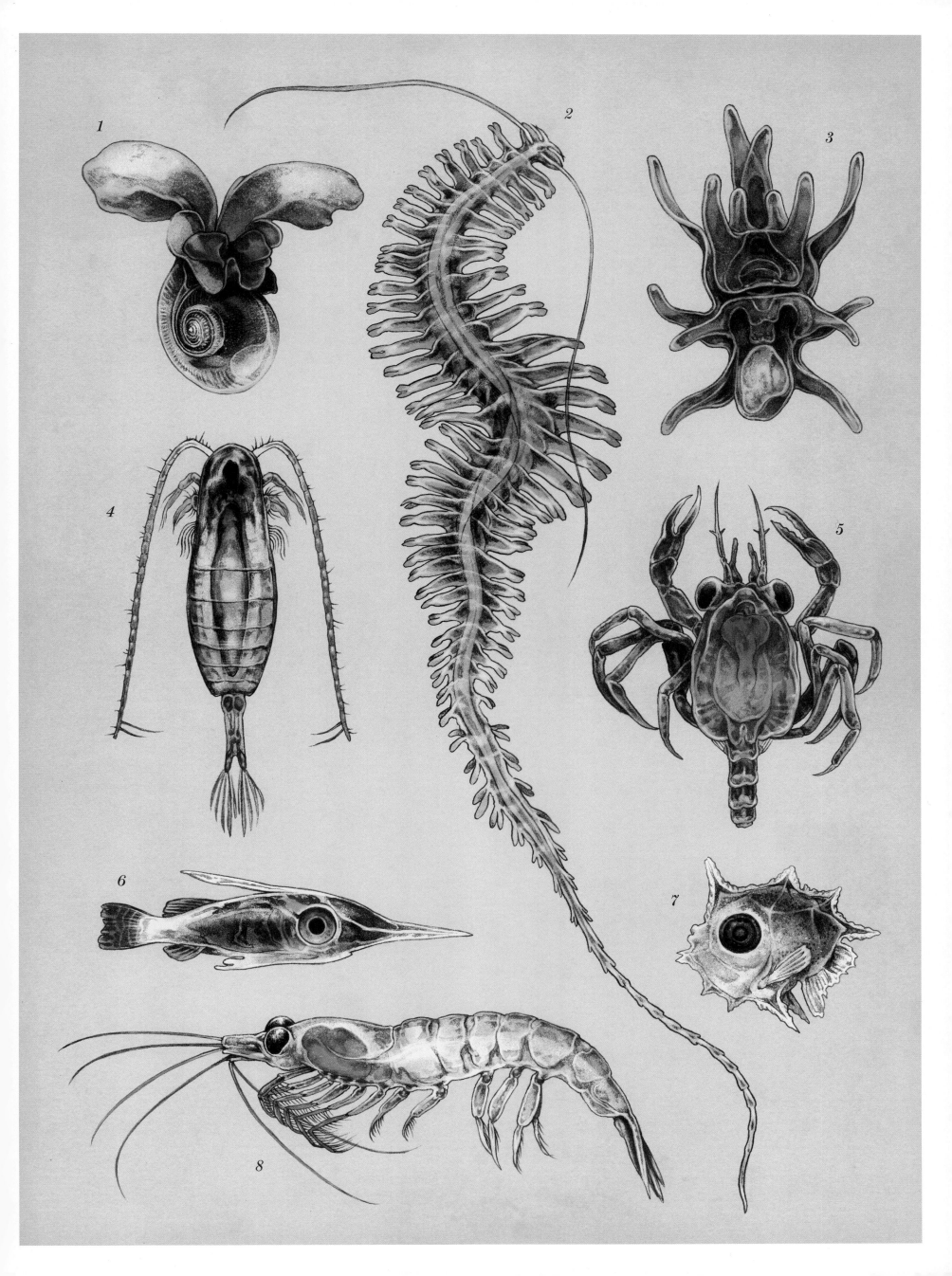

Gallery 2

Cnidaria

Jellyfish

Portuguese Man-of-War

Anemones

Habitat: Coral Reef

Jellyfish

Jellyfish are wanderers of the ocean, drifting with the currents wherever the water takes them. Despite their name, they are not fish at all, as they lack a skeleton, making them invertebrates. Their soft bodies (called bells) are around 95 percent water and contain neither brain nor heart. Without a skeleton, they have only limited movement, but they can propel themselves gently through the water by filling their body with water and squeezing it back out again.

Along with coral and anemones, jellyfish belong to the phylum Cnidaria. These animals have stinging cells used to catch prey and provide defense. Most jellyfish have long tentacles lined with cnidocytes that they dangle beneath them to catch prey. Each cnidocyte consists of a coiled, harpoon-like stinger that fires venom into the victim the moment they brush against it. Several species are translucent, meaning other animals will not see the danger ahead until it is too late, whereas others use bright colors to attract prey. For instance, flower hat jellyfish have fluorescent-tipped tentacles that may look like green algae to unsuspecting fish. The fish approach the tentacles in the hope of food but instead swim into a fatal trap. Incredibly, some animals seek out these tentacles intentionally; for example, juvenile fish and crabs sometimes take shelter within them as a means of avoiding predators. They rely on a thick mucus coating to protect them from getting stung, or nimbly dodge the tentacles as they sway in the water.

Jellyfish are known to gather in huge numbers known as blooms. These swarm-like groups occur naturally but are increasing in frequency and size every year. In some cases, blooms have been big enough to weigh down fishing nets and sink boats. The rising numbers of blooms could be a result of overfishing. Evidence suggests that when small fish are overharvested, jellyfish have no competition for food and quickly reproduce. If overfishing cannot be managed, a jellyfish-filled ocean may be in the future for our planet!

───────────────── *Key to plate* ─────────────────

1: **Box jellyfish**
Chironex fleckeri
Bell diameter: Up to 14 inches/
35 centimeters
Tentacle length: Up to 10 feet/3 meters
Also known as the sea wasp, this species has such a powerful venom that it can kill a person if untreated.

2: **Lion's mane jellyfish**
Cyanea capillata
Bell diameter: More than 6½ feet/
2 meters
Tentacle length: Up to 120 feet/
37 meters
This is the largest known species of jellyfish.

3: **Common kingslayer**
Malo kingi
Bell height: Approx. 1 inch/
3 centimeters
Tentacle length: Up to 39 inches/
100 centimeters

This tiny box jellyfish is highly venomous, and its sting can be fatal.

4: **White-spotted jellyfish**
Phyllorhiza punctata
Bell diameter: 20 inches/
50 centimeters
Tentacle length: 24 inches/
60 centimeters
Native to Australia and Japan, this species has been accidentally introduced to other areas including Hawaii and Mexico.

5: **Pacific sea nettle**
Chrysaora fuscescens
Bell diameter: Up to 12 inches/
30 centimeters
Tentacle length: Up to 15 feet/
4.5 meters
Sea nettles provide shelter for young fish and crabs.

6: **Flower hat jellyfish**
Olindias formosus
Bell diameter: Approx. 6 inches/
15 centimeters
This species lives near the seafloor and has tentacles all over its bell.

7: **Kaleidoscope jellyfish**
Haliclystus auricula
Height: Up to 1 inch/2.5 centimeters, including tentacles
This jellyfish spends its whole life in one place, attached to seagrass or seaweed by its slender stalk.

8: **Upside-down jellyfish**
Cassiopea andromeda
Bell diameter: 14 inches/
36 centimeters
Tentacle length: 14 inches/
36 centimeters
This peculiar species sits upside down on the seabed with its tentacles waving above it.

Portuguese Man-of-War

The extraordinary man-of-war is a peculiar-looking creature. Drifting partially submerged in the water, it moves by catching the wind in its sail-like body, which is filled with gas, allowing it to wander wherever the wind and ocean currents take it. Below the water's tranquil surface, a tangle of stinging tentacles trails up to 164 feet/50 meters deep. This creature is found throughout the world's warmer ocean regions and has been observed in groups of around one thousand individuals.

Although similar in appearance to jellyfish, the Portuguese man-of-war is in fact a colony made up of four types of tiny living organisms called polyps. Each polyp type has a role to play, and all of them work together to behave as one animal known as a siphonophore. These polyps include the pneumatophore, or float, which prevents the man-of-war from sinking; the long tentacles, which provide defense and catch prey; and the digestive polyps, essential for breaking down food. Each man-of-war is either male or female and produces either sperm or eggs. When the sperm and egg meet in the water, a new polyp known as a protozooid is formed, which then generates all parts of the colony.

Despite its seemingly peaceful lifestyle, the Portuguese man-of-war is a highly venomous predator, with a sting strong enough to paralyze small fish and cause painful welts on human skin. Just like a true jellyfish, the man-of-war spends most of its life in open water, but after storms it can drift near beaches. Survival is particularly difficult near the shore, because its soft body is unable to withstand collisions with rocks and the seabed. It is in shallow waters that people are most likely to come into contact with this venomous ocean wanderer.

The man-of-war does have predators, despite its formidable defenses. With thick skin and a tough mouth, loggerhead turtles can consume a whole man-of-war in one bite, without fear of being stung. The blue dragon sea slug also feeds on the man-of-war via a different method. It swims beneath the tentacles, slowly eating them before consuming the pneumatophore. Amazingly, these tiny slugs select the strongest stinging polyps and store them in their own bodies to use as a defense against predators.

Key to plate

1: Portuguese man-of-war
Physalia physalis
Pneumatophore length: Up to
12 inches/30 centimeters
Tentacle length: Up to 164 feet/
50 meters
The name Portuguese man-of-war is thought to come from its resemblance to a Portuguese warship at full sail.

2: Man-of-war fish
Nomeus gronovii
Length: Up to 15 inches/
39 centimeters
This small, agile fish manages to live among the tentacles of the Portuguese man-of-war. With a higher than usual number of vertebrae, it can twist and turn more easily than other fish, allowing it to avoid the strongest stings.

3: Detail of coiled tentacles
These long, coiled tentacles contain the stinging polyps responsible for catching prey as well as defending the colony from predators. Typically, the tentacles reach around 30 feet/
9 meters in length, but can grow up to 164 feet/50 meters, forming a trap for unsuspecting prey, such as small fish, squid, and plankton.

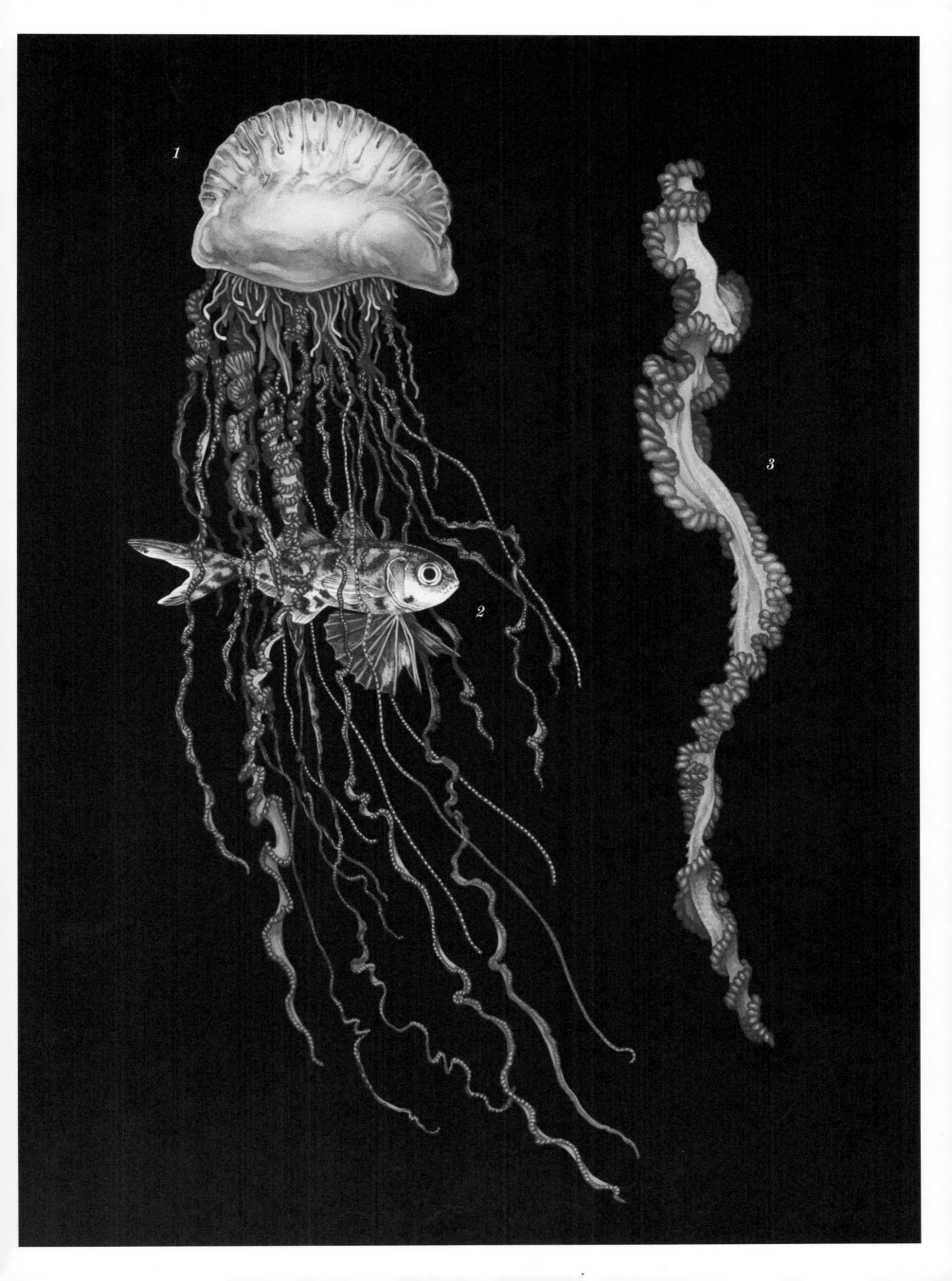

Anemones

With around one thousand known species worldwide, anemones can be found throughout the ocean, from shallow coastal areas to the deep sea, and even on the underside of Antarctic sea ice. These beautiful creatures spend most of their lives in one place, sticking to a suitable rock with a strong adhesive foot. With their colorful tentacles stretched out in the current to catch food, they can appear to be more plant than animal.

Anemones are carnivores and use their tentacles to sting and catch prey that drift, swim, or crawl too close. Similar to other members of their family (such as jellyfish), anemones have cells called cnidocytes that can deliver a sting powerful enough to kill their prey and may cause a painful rash on human skin. The strength of the sting varies, with some species able to catch and kill tiny plankton and others able to snare larger prey, such as fish.

While anemones' stinging tentacles are a danger to their prey, some creatures find shelter among them. With a thick layer of sting-proof mucus, clownfish live within the bubble-tip anemone, where they are safe from predators. In return, the anemone is kept clean by the family of clownfish, who rid it of parasites. Relationships can exist between anemones and other animals, too. The pompom crab picks up and holds tiny anemones in its claws. The anemones are carried by the crab to areas of the ocean that would otherwise be unreachable, and the crab can wave the anemones at predators to protect itself.

Key to plate

1: **Bubble-tip anemone**
Entacmaea quadricolor
Diameter: Up to 12 inches/
30 centimeters
This beautiful anemone provides
a home for clownfish.

2: **Hell's fire anemone**
Actinodendron plumosum
Diameter: Up to 12 inches/
30 centimeters
As the name suggests, this anemone
can deliver a painful sting causing skin
ulcers in humans.

3: **Jewel anemone**
Corynactis viridis
Diameter: Up to $^2/_5$ inch/1 centimeter
These tiny anemones group together
and grow in large numbers.

4: **Snakelocks anemone**
Anemonia viridis
Diameter: Up to 3 inches/
8 centimeters

Microscopic algae called zooxanthellae
live inside the tentacles of this species,
providing its color and extra food
through photosynthesis.

5: **Edwardsiella andrillae**
Length: Up to 1 inch/2.5 centimeters
The only anemone to be found
living in the ice of Antarctica, it was
discovered by an underwater robot
in 2010.

6: **Fish-eating anemone**
Urticina piscivora
Diameter: Up to 10 inches/
25 centimeters
Unlike most other anemones, this
species can detach quite easily from
rocks and will readily move in search of
food or if threatened.

7: **Strawberry anemone**
Actinia fragacea
Diameter: Up to 4 inches/
10 centimeters

This shore-dwelling anemone tucks
its tentacles in when exposed to air,
which leaves it looking much like a
strawberry on the rocks!

8: **Parasitic anemone**
Calliactis parasitica
Diameter: Up to 2 inches/
5 centimeters
Often found living on the shells of
hermit crabs, parasitic anemones
benefit from a free ride to new areas
of food, while the crabs gain protection
from the anemones' tentacles.

9: **Venus flytrap anemone**
Actinoscyphia aurelia
Height: Up to 12 inches/30 centimeters
This deep-sea anemone bears
resemblance to the Venus flytrap plant.
It uses its long stalk to turn and face the
current, making it easier to catch food.

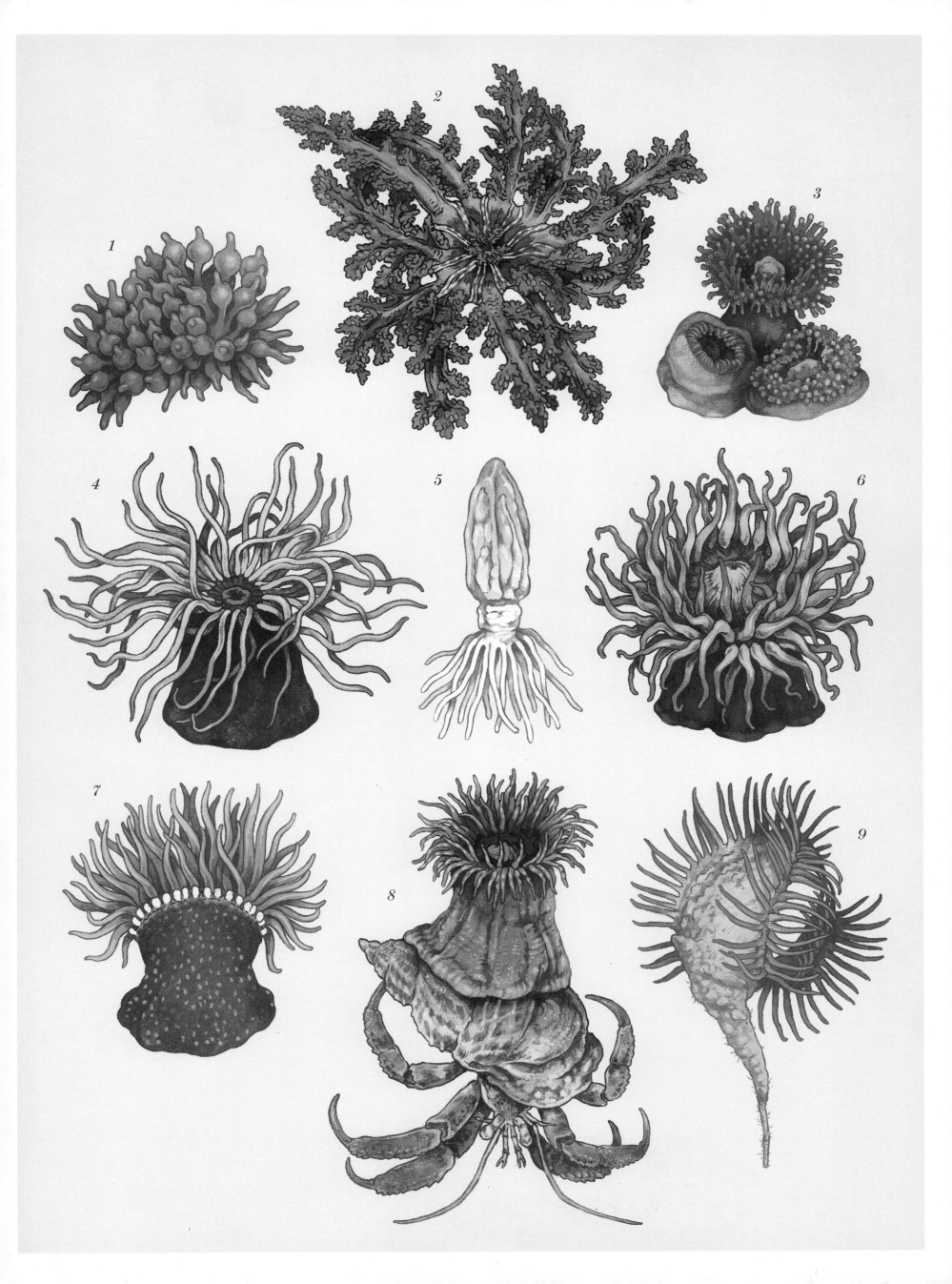

Habitat: Coral Reef

Vibrant and bustling with life, this habitat is like an underwater metropolis, supporting an incredible 25 percent of marine life worldwide. The animals that live here seek shelter in the reef's nooks and crannies, find camouflage against its bright backdrop, and feast on an abundant supply of food within its colorful corridors.

Coral reefs are formed by coral polyps: tiny animals that resemble sea anemones and live in huge groups called colonies. When they die, the polyps leave behind their hard calcium carbonate (limestone) skeletons, and the reef gradually becomes bigger. Coral polyps find food by waving their tentacles in the water to catch drifting scraps. They also get nutrients from microscopic algae called zooxanthellae, which live inside the polyps themselves and make food using energy from the sun (via photosynthesis). Zooxanthellae produce pigments that give coral reefs their characteristic bright colors, and several million can be found in just one square inch of coral. Coral reefs are the largest living structures on our planet. They make up enormous habitats such as the Belize Barrier Reef in Central America and the Great Barrier Reef in Australia, which are so big, they are visible from space.

These complex habitats only grow under specific conditions, requiring temperatures of 68 to 90°F/20 to 32°C and shallow, sunlit waters. Such conditions vary naturally with our planet's cycles, but they are altering more dramatically due to climate change. If sea temperatures rise, the zooxanthellae cannot survive, so they leave the polyps. The corals then lose their color and most of their food, and the whole habitat is threatened. It's not just marine species that this will impact. Coral reefs are also an important resource for humans; in addition to being a thriving habitat for our food sources, coral reefs are home to organisms whose unique chemical compounds are being studied for treatment of infections, heart disease, and even cancer.

Key to plate

Belize Barrier Reef, Central America

1: Reef manta ray
Mobula alfredi
Width: Approx. 11½ feet/3.5 meters
This is the second largest species
of ray in the world.

2: Green turtle
Chelonia mydas
Length: Approx. 3½ feet/1.1 meters
This turtle takes its name from
the color of its skin and fat rather
than the color of its shell.

3: Common bottlenose dolphin
Tursiops truncatus
Length: Up to 13 feet/4 meters
This species lives in social groups
called pods. They can contain as
many as 1,000 individuals.

4: Staghorn coral
Acropora cervicornis
Height: Up to 4 feet/1.2 meters
This coral grows faster than most,
adding as much as 8 inches/20
centimeters a year.

5: Blue chromis
Chromis cyanea
Length: Up to 6 inches/15 centimeters
Normally found in big shoals, these
bright fish live near branching coral
when they are young and are always
ready to dart for shelter if threatened.

6: Table coral
Acropora cytherea
Diameter: Up to 6½ feet/2 meters
Growing in flat, table-like structures,
this coral gives prey animals shelter
from predators hunting above.

7: Brain coral
Diploria labyrinthiformis
Diameter: Up to 6½ feet/2 meters
The brain coral's polyps sit protected
within its mazelike grooves and folds.

8: Spotted moray eel
Gymnothorax moringa
Length: Approx. 24 inches/
60 centimeters
This solitary eel lives in crevices
in the reef. It normally hides away
with only its head poking out.

9: Caesar grunt
Haemulon carbonarium
Length: Up to 8 inches/20 centimeters
This family of fish, called grunts, make
noises underwater by grinding their
teeth.

Gallery 3

Mollusks and Echinoderms

Bivalves

Gastropods

Cephalopods

Echinoderms

Habitat: Deep Sea

Bivalves

With a hinged shell made of two halves, bivalves are an interesting type of mollusk that is able to completely enclose itself in an armored cocoon, impenetrable to most predators. Bivalves are found throughout the ocean and can survive in some of the toughest habitats on earth, including deep-sea hydrothermal vents, which reach temperatures in excess of 572°F/300°C.

Bivalves are attached to the seabed usually by a tough, stringy material called byssal thread, and they don't move much after they have settled. Instead of hunting for food, they filter feed using tiny hairs called cilia to catch passing plankton. This method of feeding enables bivalves to also filter the water, making it cleaner for other animals and plants. Some species of bivalve provide a habitat for other creatures, too—beds of mussels can support a variety of living things including seaweeds, worms, small fish, and crabs.

Perhaps the most coveted feature of the bivalves is their ability to create nacre. This shimmering material is more commonly known as pearl or mother-of-pearl, and is the only jewel on earth created by an animal. Nacre is secreted as a form of defense—it smooths the inside of bivalves' shells, protecting their soft bodies from invasive parasites and other harmful intruders. If a parasite does make its way inside, layers of nacre will grow to protect the bivalve and, eventually, form a pearl. Only one in approximately ten thousand wild oysters will create a natural pearl.

Aside from use in jewelry, some bivalves have been cultivated for centuries for people to eat. For example, there is evidence that oysters were cultivated for consumption in ancient Rome. Today, oysters remain a very popular seafood and are harvested from the open ocean by either dredging or handpicking or they are farmed in designated parts of the ocean.

Key to plate

1: Common mussel
Mytilus edulis
Length: Up to 4 inches/10 centimeters
These mussels usually grow in clumps, attaching themselves to rocks or one another by byssal threads.

2: Queen scallop
Aequipecten opercularis
Length: Up to 3½ inches/
9 centimeters
The queen scallop swims by sucking in and releasing water using a valve, which propels them forward.

3: Flame shell
Limaria hians
Length: Approx. 1 inch/2.5 centimeters
Named for its bright fringe of tentacles, this bivalve's shell is always slightly open, ready to catch food.

4: Pacific oyster
Magallana gigas
Length: Up to 10 inches/
25 centimeters
Originating from Japan, these animals are now farmed around the world.

5: Common cockle
Cerastoderma edule
Length: Up to 2 inches/5 centimeters
Cockle shells were used to make wavy patterns in prehistoric clay work known as Cardium pottery.

6: Fan mussel
Atrina fragilis
Length: Up to 19 inches/
48 centimeters
This rare species buries the narrow portion of its shell in the seabed, leaving the wider end out to feed.

7: Giant clam
Tridacna gigas
Length: Approx. 4 feet/1.2 meters
Giant clams are the largest known species of bivalve and can live for around 100 years.

8: Razor clam
Ensis magnus
Length: Approx. 6 inches/
15 centimeters
All razor clams dig into the sand, preferring to leave just their siphon out in the water to breathe. When burrowing, they can produce an impressive spout of water, which gives them the nickname of "spoots" in the United Kingdom.

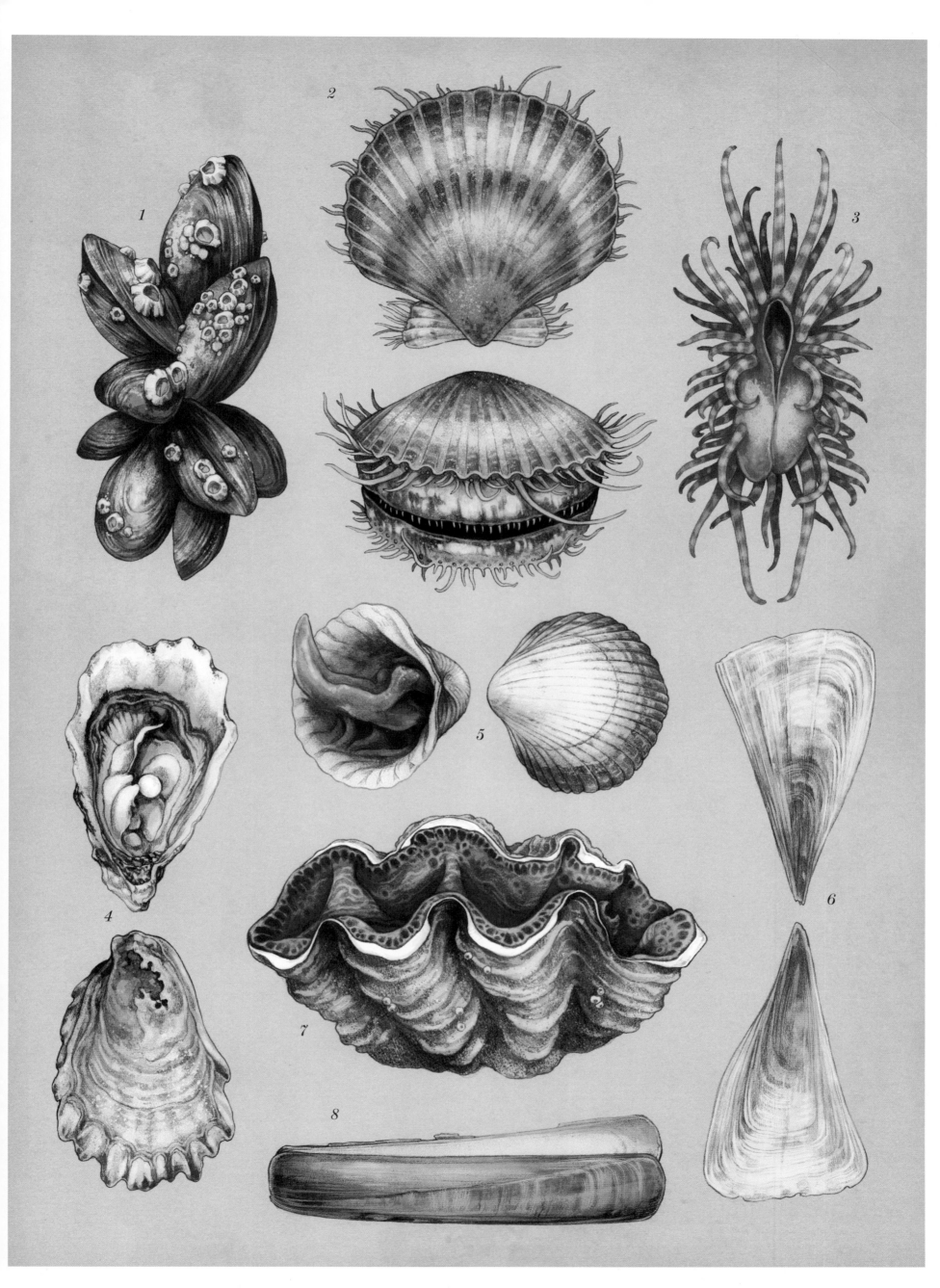

Gastropods

More commonly known as slugs and snails, gastropods (whose name means "stomach foot") are mollusks. They are the only members of this group to successfully live on land as well as in both salt water and fresh water. Scientists estimate that there are around 65,000 species of marine gastropods, with the largest—the Australian trumpet snail—reaching nearly 3 feet/1 meter long, and the smallest—the micro-mollusks—reaching only a few millimeters.

Typically, snails have coiled shells that protect them from predators. Made from calcium carbonate, a material found in rocks, these shells are strong and durable and will often last long after the animal that made them has died. The discarded shells sometimes become homes for other animals, such as hermit crabs and worms, but will eventually break down into grains of sand to form beaches.

Sea slugs and the closely related sea hares have beautiful colors, patterns, and sensory horns called rhinophores, which make them fascinating underwater creatures to observe. Though they lack a shell, they are by no means defenseless. Some, such as the blue dragon, can eat animals too dangerous for others to tackle, like jellyfish. In doing so, they steal the venom for their own defense. It is because of this that the striking colors found on sea slugs often serve as a stark warning to predators.

Gastropod diets vary between being herbivorous, carnivorous, and omnivorous. Some species are predatory, while others scavenge, and some are parasitic—feeding on the bodies of other living creatures. All gastropods eat using a toothlike mouth called a radula, which is specially adapted to the eating habits of each species. Drill-shaped radulae make tiny holes in the shell of their victim, allowing the gastropod to squirt stomach acids inside and, later, suck out the dissolved meal. Other gastropods are grazers and have radulae better suited to scraping algae from rocks.

Key to plate

1: **Blue dragon**
Glaucus atlanticus
Length: Up to 1 inch/3 centimeters
This slug hangs beneath the Portuguese man-of-war, feeding on its stinging cells.

2: **Textile cone**
Conus textile
Length: Up to 4 inches/10 centimeters
Highly predatory and venomous, textile cone shells use their modified radula to fire deadly stings.

3: **Tiger cowrie**
Cypraea tigris
Length: Up to 6 inches/15 centimeters
Cowries can pull their soft bodies inside their shell when in danger.

4: **Sea hare**
Aplysia punctata
Length: Up to 3 inches/7 centimeters
The color of these animals varies with their diet, which consists of red and green algae.

5: **Common limpet**
Patella vulgata
Diameter: Up to 2 inches/
6 centimeters
The limpet's thick, conical shell offers a strong defense against predators and powerful waves.

6: **Anna's chromodoris**
Chromodoris annae
Length: Up to 2 inches/5 centimeters
This colorful sea slug eats certain species of poisonous sponge.

7: **Alabaster murex**
Siratus alabaster
Length: Up to 9 inches/22 centimeters
The spines covering this snail's exterior protect it from predators.

8: **Violet sea snail**
Janthina janthina
Length: Up to 2 inches/4 centimeters
Floating from a raft of self-made bubbles, this small snail hangs upside down at the water's surface.

9: **Queen conch**
Lobatus gigas
Length: Up to 12 inches/
30 centimeters
The shells of this snail have been used as hornlike musical instruments by humans for more than 10,000 years.

Cephalopods

Cephalopods are a group of highly intelligent invertebrates that include octopuses, cuttlefish, and squid. From the tiny blue-ringed octopus to the mysterious Humboldt squid, these remarkable animals exhibit a huge range of lifestyles, habitats, and complex behaviors.

The Greek translation of the word *cephalopod* is "head foot," which describes the way these creatures appear to have their heads attached to their many limbs. Cephalopods are soft-bodied animals, with strong muscles to control their multiple arms. Despite their jellylike appearance, they have a toughened beak in their mouth that is strong enough to pierce the shells of crabs and lobsters—their preferred prey. Many of these animals also possess a toxin that paralyzes their victim, allowing it to be eaten safely. In some species, such as the blue-ringed octopus, this toxin is extremely potent—one bite has enough venom to kill several humans.

Cephalopods have three hearts and blue, copper-based blood called hemocyanin. Their arms (with suckers) and tentacles (without suckers) are used to catch food and to move things around their habitat. These limbs are incredibly dexterous—the coconut octopus will even use its suckers to hold on to the insides of empty coconut shells while it tucks itself safely inside.

Intelligence is a key feature of the cephalopod, too. Octopuses are particularly smart, and research has proven that they are able to problem solve and remember solutions. They can be highly efficient escape artists who, aided by their lack of bones, can squeeze their whole body through the tiniest of spaces to evade danger. Their skin also contains color-changing pigment cells that allow them to camouflage with their environment. If none of these defenses works, octopuses can produce a dark cloud of ink that acts as a decoy and allows for a quick getaway.

Key to plate

1: Hummingbird bobtail squid
Euprymna berryi
Mantle (body) length: Up to 2 inches/
5 centimeters
This tiny squid has a symbiotic relationship with the glowing bacterium *V. fischeri*, helping it to camouflage.

2: Dumbo octopus
Grimpoteuthis bathynectes
Mantle length: Unknown
This is one of the deepest-dwelling octopuses we know of, and it is incredibly rare.

3: Flamboyant cuttlefish
Metasepia pfefferi
Mantle length: Approx. 2 inches/
6 centimeters
This cuttlefish doesn't swim as much as other species but crawls along the ocean floor instead.

4: Knobbed argonaut
Argonauta nodosa
Length: Up to 1 inch/3 centimeters (males), 12 inches/30 centimeters (females)
These fragile-looking animals are known as paper nautiluses but are in fact octopuses. The females secrete a paper-thin shell to live in and to hold their eggs while they grow.

5: Giant Pacific octopus
Enteroctopus dofleini
Mantle length: Up to 24 inches/
60 centimeters
The largest known species of octopus, this giant can weigh up to 200 pounds/
91 kilograms.

6: Chambered nautilus
Nautilus pompilius

Mantle length: Up to 8 inches/
20 centimeters
These deep-sea creatures occupy the innermost chamber of their shell when first hatched and move into larger segments as they grow.

7: Humboldt squid
Dosidicus gigas
Mantle length: Approx. 5 feet/
1.5 meters
This species is also known as the red devil, due to its bioluminescent light.

8: Greater blue-ringed octopus
Hapalochlaena lunulata
Mantle length: Up to 2 inches/
4 centimeters
The blue rings on this tiny octopus flash brightly when approached, warning of a deadly bite.

Echinoderms

Found in every part of the ocean, from the shallows to the deep sea, echinoderms either creep slowly over the seabed or are anchored in one place, gently sifting food from the surrounding water. In appearance, this group, which includes sea stars, sea cucumbers, sea urchins, and sand dollars, can seem passive and defenseless, unable to chase prey or evade capture. However, these creatures are full of surprises. They are in fact amazing predators, capable of living in some of the most extreme environments on the planet.

With a name meaning "spiny skin," echinoderms usually have a covering of tough spines that helps to protect them from predators. In addition to these spines, sucker-like protrusions known as tube feet also cover their undersides. They help echinoderms to stick to, or crawl along, the seabed and also grab hold of food. Tube feet can smell and taste the water around them, providing vital sensory information that can lead echinoderms toward food sources and away from predators.

By positioning themselves in places where they can catch ocean currents, echinoderms have many inventive ways of feeding. Sea cucumbers munch through the seabed, digesting any food they find and excreting clean sand in long coils behind them. Sea urchins use a different method: with five tough plates in their mouth, known as Aristotle's lantern, they scrape algae from rocks. Sea stars prey on many creatures including sea snails, which they pull off rocks to get to the flesh inside. Unlike most other animals, sea stars can take their stomachs out of their bodies, allowing them to digest food that does not fit in their mouths. This is important for an animal without teeth with which to chew a large meal.

Echinoderms have equally inventive ways of defending themselves. Some crawl away, while others, like the sea cucumber, eject their digestive system, leaving it behind as a decoy. Incredibly, echinoderms can also regrow body parts lost to predators, and sea stars can regenerate whole limbs. A single arm can regrow into a complete animal because it contains everything a sea star needs to survive.

--- *Key to plate* ---

1: **Crown-of-thorns sea star**
Acanthaster planci
Diameter: Up to 14 inches/
35 centimeters
These spiny-looking sea stars have up to twenty-one arms.

2: **Sea pig**
Scotoplanes globosa
Length: Up to 6 inches/15 centimeters
These sea cucumbers appear to walk along the ocean floor using long, tubelike limbs.

3: **Red slate pencil urchin**
Heterocentrotus mammillatus
Diameter: Up to 3 inches/
8 centimeters
Thick, broad spines are characteristic of this group. The color and thickness vary depending on their habitat.

4: **Crimson knobbed sea star**
Protoreaster linckii
Diameter: Up to 12 inches/
30 centimeters
An impressive predator, this sea star eats clams, oysters, and mussels as well as other sea stars.

5: **Rosy feather star**
Antedon bifida
Diameter: Up to 8 inches/
20 centimeters
Feather stars are in a class called the crinoids. Their feather-like arms catch plankton in the passing water.

6: **Leopard sea cucumber**
Bohadschia argus
Length: Up to 24 inches/
60 centimeters
This sea cucumber often has a small fish called a pearl fish living inside it.

7: **Spiny brittle star**
Ophiothrix spiculata
Diameter: Up to 5 inches/
12 centimeters
These brittle stars tend to be small but occur in large numbers.

8: **Blue sea star**
Linckia laevigata
Diameter: Up to 12 inches/
30 centimeters
A tiny parasitic snail is often found on the skin of this species.

9: **Eccentric sand dollar**
Dendraster excentricus
Diameter: Approx. 3 inches/
8 centimeters
Sand dollars are flat, burrowing sea urchins. Their larvae can clone themselves, reducing their chances of being eaten by predators.

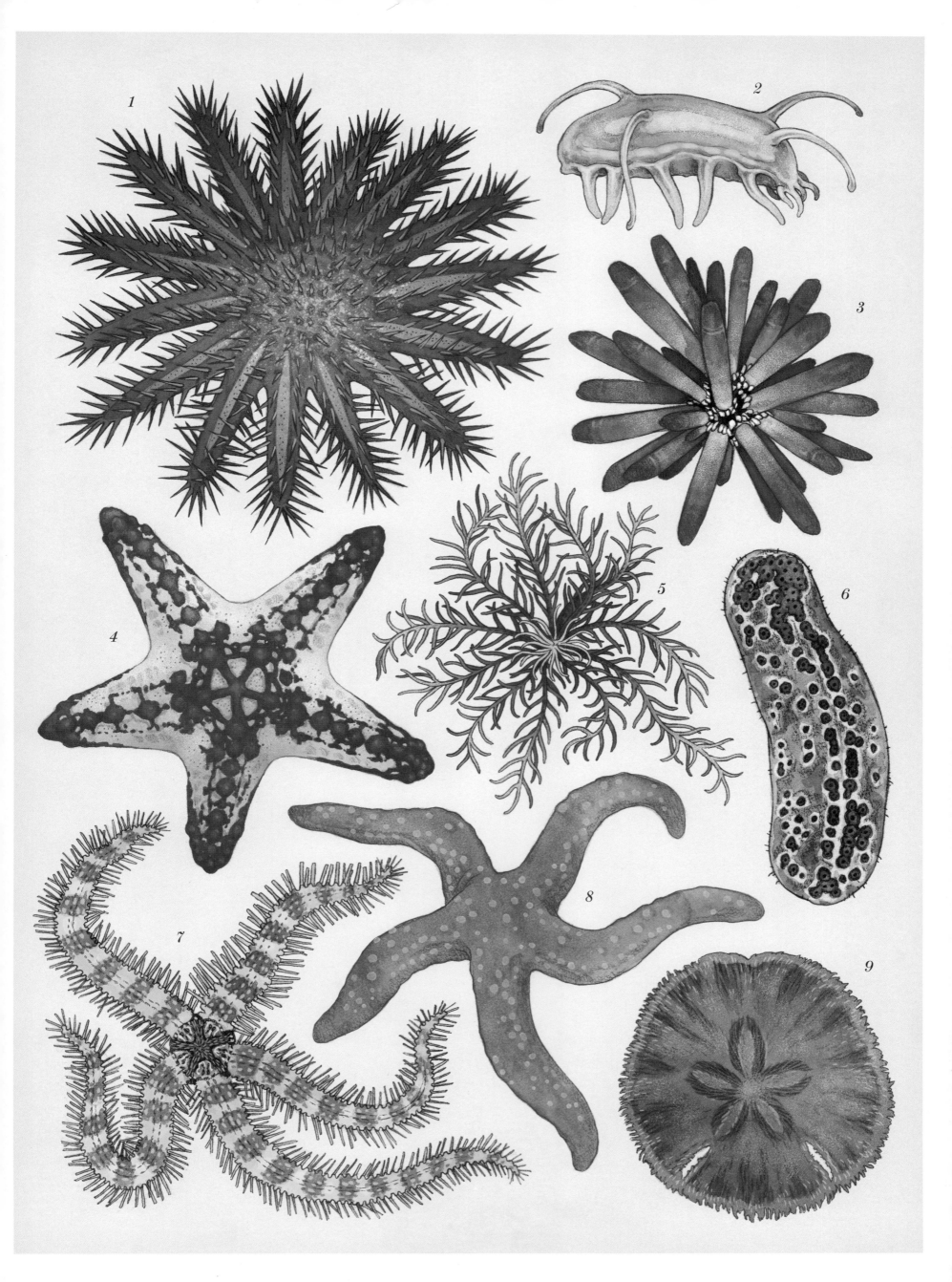

Habitat: Deep Sea

The deep sea is an alien, inhospitable place: it is constantly dark and cold, and the pressure is strong enough to crush most creatures. For a long time, people thought nothing could live here—but with the use of underwater vehicles, scientists have discovered life throughout the ocean's depths and documented species whose features and behaviors enable them to survive in the most hostile conditions on earth.

Because no light reaches the seafloor, no plants or algae can grow there, so herbivores can't survive. The only way to feed is by scavenging, hunting, or sieving tiny particles of food from the water. Most food drifts down from the surface, including fragments of algae, dead animals, and other organic waste—it can take weeks to sink to the seabed. These soft flakes of "marine snow" are vital for the diet of many deep-sea creatures. Occasionally, a real feast such as a whale carcass falls from the surface. Animals that may have gone for days without food will not let anything go to waste. Scavengers such as giant isopods, hagfish, and sharks cover the carcass and eat all the meat in a few months. What is left sinks into the seabed to be broken down by bacteria, leaving behind just the bones. Even these provide nutrients for tiny creatures that worm inside them to get to the fats and proteins.

Most of the time, however, animals must hunt for food, which can be a challenge in the dark waters. Many animals get around this problem by making their own light, a feature called bioluminescence. This is done either by chemicals inside their bodies or via bacteria that live on them. Almost 90 percent of creatures that live in open water are bioluminescent, and most of these can be found in the deep sea, providing the only light visible in the inky depths. Though bioluminescence can allow predators to see in the dark, it more often attracts smaller fish toward hungry mouths. Other animals use light to communicate, flashing messages to each other through the gloom.

Key to plate

Abyssal plain, Atlantic Ocean

1: **Atolla jellyfish**
Atolla wyvillei
Bell diameter: Up to 7 inches/
17 centimeters
When under attack, the atolla flashes blue. This attracts larger predators, which usually eat the original attacker—allowing the atolla to escape.

2: **Common northern comb jelly**
Bolinopsis infundibulum
Length: Up to 6 inches/15 centimeters
This predator hunts tiny zooplankton.

3: **Black dragonfish**
Idiacanthus atlanticus
Length: Approx. 16 inches/

40 centimeters (females),
2 inches/5 centimeters (males)
This fish makes red bioluminescence. Most deep-sea animals can't see red, so the dragonfish can go unseen.

4: **Bluntnose sixgill shark**
Hexanchus griseus
Length: Up to 16 feet/5 meters
The sixgill is thought to resemble sharks from 200 million years ago.

5: **Humpback anglerfish**
Melanocetus johnsonii
Length: Approx. 7 inches/
18 centimeters (females), 1 inch/
3 centimeters (males)
The females of this species have a bright lure to attract prey, and a huge mouth and stomach.

6: **Bone-eating snot flower worm**
Osedax mucofloris
Length: Approx. $^2/_5$ inch/1 centimeter
Female worms bore into fallen whale bones to eat the marrow inside. Microscopic males live inside females.

7: **Atlantic hagfish**
Myxine glutinosa
Length: Up to 16 inches/
40 centimeters
This carrion feeder can produce slimy mucus, clogging the gills of any attacker.

8: **Giant isopod**
Bathynomus giganteus
Length: Up to 14 inches/
36 centimeters
This giant arthropod can go for weeks or even months without food.

Gallery 4

Arthropods

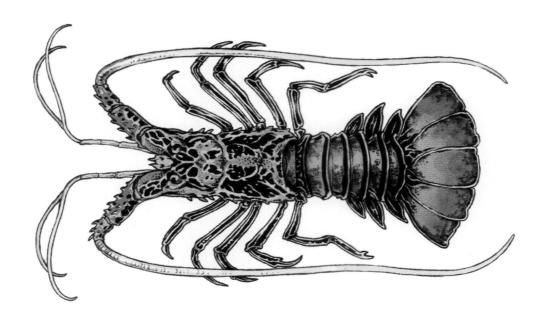

Crustaceans
Peacock Mantis Shrimp
Habitat: Tide Pool

Crustaceans

Crustaceans are members of a group called the arthropods, which include insects and arachnids. These are some of the most successful animals that have ever lived on our planet and, in fact, account for around 80 percent of all known living species.

With bodies arranged in segments (the thorax, abdomen, and head), crustaceans have different limb pairs associated with varying roles. Some are used for walking and swimming, others for catching and cutting food, and some for sensing the environment. Crustaceans can also "taste" with their feet and detect chemicals from other animals in the water. These senses allow crustaceans to find food as well as a good home, and enable this group of animals, from microscopic copepods to hefty lobsters, to thrive in every type of ocean.

A tough, shell-like armor, or exoskeleton, covers the body of most crustaceans and protects them from predators. In order for crustaceans to grow, this exoskeleton must be shed often in a process that can take several weeks. Freshly molted crustaceans are soft and vulnerable and must hide or bury themselves until their new shell has hardened. Hermit crabs, however, have no exoskeleton on the rear half of their body, and so must find other means to protect themselves. They search the ocean floor, scavenging for discarded shells from other mollusks. Once sure that there are no other inhabitants, the hermit crab can move in and claim the shell for itself.

While most crustaceans can move around, barnacles adopt a more sedentary lifestyle. Firmly attached to the rocks, they open tiny doors in their shell-like home to feed on passing plankton. Before settling on a rock, larval barnacles will "smell" the water—the odor of other barnacles will indicate safety while that of a predatory dogwhelk will signal danger.

Key to plate

1: Painted spiny lobster
Panulirus versicolor
Length: Up to 12 inches/
30 centimeters
These beautiful lobsters are nocturnal and live alone in small caves and crevices in coral reefs.

2: Acorn barnacle
Semibalanus balanoides
Diameter: Up to 15 millimeters
This barnacle spends its whole life cemented to a rock. It is covered with tiny hairs called cirri, which capture passing plankton.

3: Norway lobster
Nephrops norvegicus
Length: Up to 8 inches/20 centimeters
The tail of this small, slim lobster is known as scampi when it's eaten.

4: Velvet swimming crab
Necora puber
Carapace width: Up to 4 inches/
10 centimeters
These crabs are particularly feisty and have red eyes, earning them the nickname "devil crab."

5: Japanese spider crab
Macrocheira kaempferi
Carapace width: 16 inches/
40 centimeters
The largest known arthropod, the long legs of this crab can grow up to 13 feet/4 meters. They often break, but can be regrown.

6: Harlequin shrimp
Hymenocera picta
Length: Up to 2 inches/5 centimeters
This species feeds exclusively on sea stars, and will work together to flip

them over, carry them back to their reef crevice, and feed on them.

7: Indo-Pacific horseshoe crab
Tachypleus gigas
Length: Up to 20 inches/
50 centimeters
The blood of this crab can release chemicals that clot blood when it becomes contaminated with a pathogen. For this reason, it is often used in human vaccine and drug trials.

8: Common hermit crab
Pagurus bernhardus
Carapace length: Approx. 1 inch/
3.5 centimeters
These crabs sometimes use discarded plastic bottles as replacement shells, but this can be disastrous, as they can become trapped inside and starve.

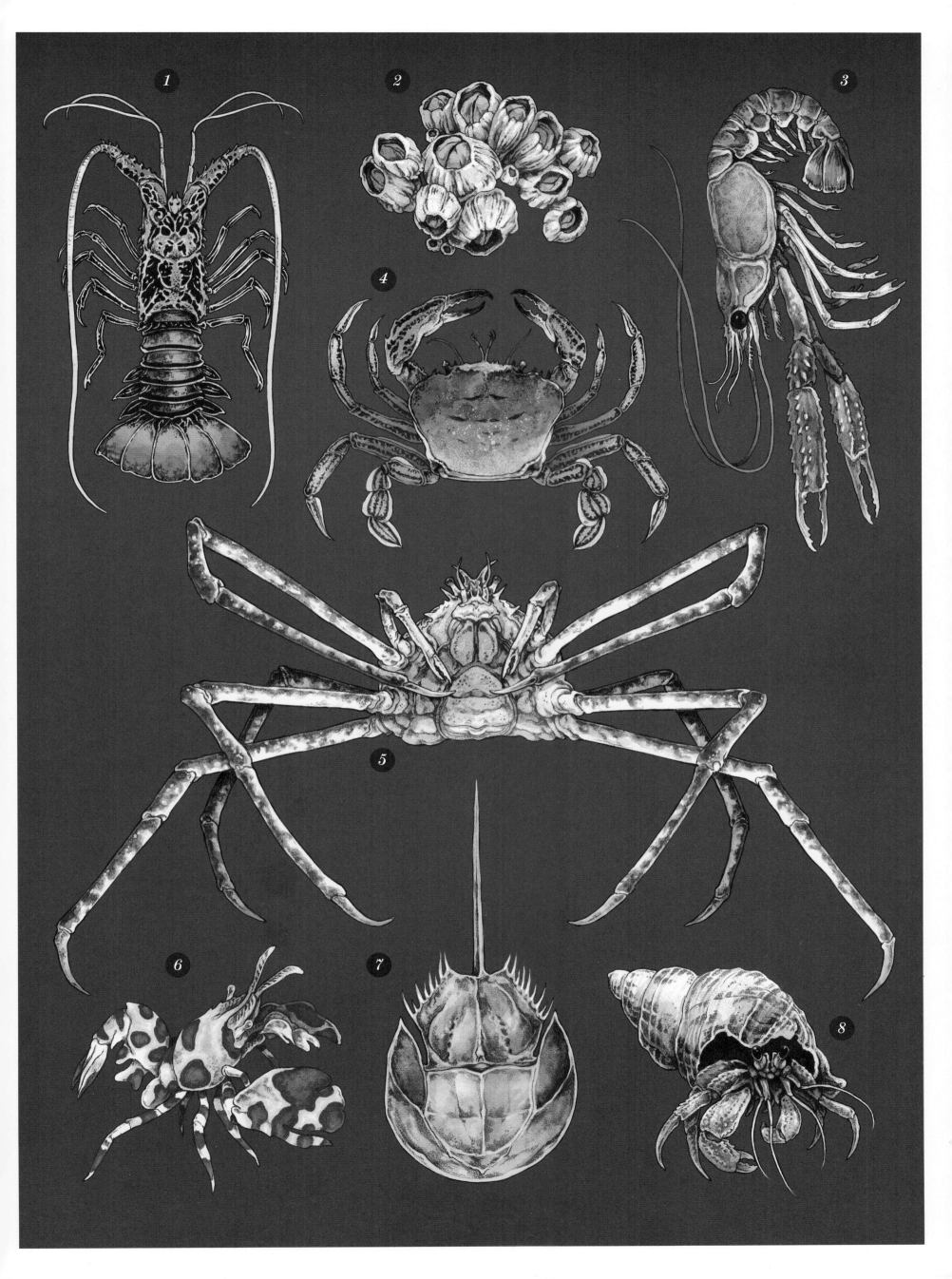

1a

1b

Peacock Mantis Shrimp

Despite their small size (typically less than 8 inches/20 centimeters), peacock mantis shrimp are incredible hunters and fierce defenders of their territories. They burrow under the sand, then lie and wait for unsuspecting prey, ambushing them with incredible force when they venture too close.

All mantis shrimp species have exceptionally powerful claws. Some use them to smash open shells, while others have spears, better for piercing softer meals such as fish. With large, club-shaped claws, the peacock mantis shrimp is a smasher, repeatedly punching its shellfish prey to get to the meat inside. Scientists have estimated the speed of the punch to be around 50 miles/80 kilometers per hour, with an acceleration rate and strike force similar to those of a bullet. Each strike has two impacts: the first from the claw hitting the prey, and the second from a phenomenon called cavitation—small gas-filled bubbles form as the claw moves through the water, then release extra heat and light energy when they collapse, helping to kill the mantis shrimp's victim.

Mantis shrimp also have some of the most complex eyes in the world. Human

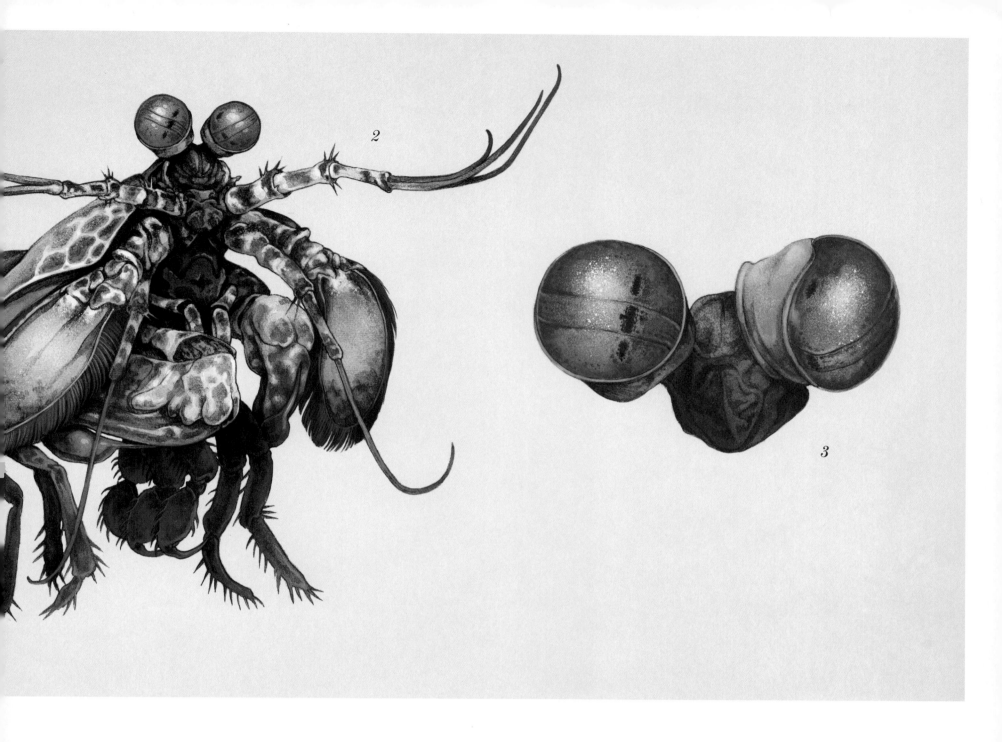

eyes have three types of light-sensitive cells called photoreceptors that tell us what color we are seeing. By comparison, mantis shrimp have between twelve and sixteen of these types, which means they can see colors we can't imagine. They use this amazing eyesight to spot their prey and also to communicate. Specialized patches on their shell reflect light in a way that only other mantis shrimp can see, meaning that these feisty shrimp can send each other signals and warnings, avoiding unnecessary conflict.

──────────────── *Key to plate* ────────────────

1a: **Claw (smasher)**
The claws of smasher mantis shrimp, such as *Odontodactylus scyllarus* (pictured), have spring-loaded joints that store energy from the muscles, and they unleash it all at once.

1b: **Claw (spearer)**
Spearer mantis shrimp have deadly sharp barbs on the end of their thin claws. This helps them to jab and snag softer prey.

2: **Peacock mantis shrimp**
Odontodactylus scyllarus
Length: Up to 7 inches/18 centimeters
There are over 400 species of mantis shrimp found throughout the world. This one is found mainly within the Indian and Pacific Oceans, and is a bright and colorful inhabitant of shallow reefs.

3: **Eyes**
Many light receptors facing in slightly different directions give the peacock mantis shrimp a large field of vision and the ability to see much faster movements than a human eye can. The black band that runs down the center shows which way the shrimp is looking.

Habitat: Tide Pool

Imagine the most changeable habitat you can, where nothing stays the same for long, including the temperature, the amount of oxygen you have to breathe, the space you can occupy, and who you share the space with. This is life in the tide pools. Formed in the holes and hollows of the shoreline, tide pools are shallow pockets of seawater left isolated from the ocean at low tide.

Tides are the rise and fall of the ocean. They are caused by the sun and moon's gravitational pull on Earth, making the ocean bulge around its middle and pulling water away from the coasts. Because the moon orbits Earth and Earth rotates on an axis, this pull works on different regions at different times, so that the tides change and move. Some places have faster tides than others because of their geography. For instance, the Bay of Fundy in Canada fills and empties a billion tons/metric tons of water at around 9 miles/15 kilometers per hour twice a day. That's much faster than most people can run!

For tide pool wildlife, it's important to be in the right place at the right time. Any creatures caught off guard by the tide risk finding themselves high and dry. To avoid this, animals carefully time their activities to fit around the tides' schedule and have a few handy backup plans, too. Limpets leave a trail of mucus (slime) behind them when they search for food at high tide. As soon as the tide starts to retreat, they can follow the trail back to the safety of the rocks, where they clamp down, locking water inside their shell. Some animals, such as blennies, have adapted so that they can survive out of the water entirely. If they stay damp and cool, they can breathe through their skin, allowing them to wriggle and hop between tide pools—useful if there is no food in their tide pool or if they get caught out of the water.

Key to plate

Tide pool at low tide, United Kingdom

1: **Montagu's blenny**
Coryphoblennius galerita
Length: Up to 3 inches/8.5 centimeters
A single crest on the head distinguishes this blenny from other species.

2: **Common limpet**
Patella vulgata
Diameter: 2 inches/6 centimeters
A limpet's radula is made of some of the toughest material known on earth.

3: **Bladder wrack**
Fucus vesiculosus
Length: Up to 39 inches/ 100 centimeters
This seaweed has air bladders that allow the fronds to float in the water, where there is the most sunlight. This helps them to stay close to the surface in order to photosynthesize.

4a: **Beadlet anemone (open)**
4b: **Beadlet anemone (closed)**
Actinia equina
Diameter: Up to 2 inches/ 5 centimeters
These territorial anemones will push away others that settle too close.

5: **Two-spotted goby**
Gobiusculus flavescens
Length: Up to 2 inches/6 centimeters
This species swims above the seaweed rather than sheltering under rocks.

6: **Common sea star**
Asterias rubens
Diameter: Up to 20 inches/ 52 centimeters
These sea stars are experts at opening shellfish using their tube feet.

7: **Light bulb sea squirt**
Clavelina lepadiformis
Height: Up to 4/5 inch/2 centimeters

These tube-shaped animals have a notochord (the beginnings of a spine) when they are larvae, but the adults remain invertebrates.

8: **Common periwinkle**
Littorina littorea
Height: Up to 2 inches/5 centimeters
This sea snail can often be found in clusters around tide pools at low tide.

9: **Green crab**
Carcinus maenas
Carapace width: Up to 3½ inches/ 9 centimeters
European natives, these common crabs are considered invasive in the Americas, Australia, and New Zealand.

Gallery 5

Fish

Coral Reef Fish
Seahorses and Pipefish
Rays and Skates
Sharks
Whale Shark
Habitat: Mangrove Forest

Coral Reef Fish

Coral reef fish inhabit one of the most diverse and beautiful ecosystems in the ocean—the coral reef. This is also one of the rarest habitats, requiring very specific conditions to grow and thrive (see page 22). The animals that call the reef home are there for a variety of reasons, but all of them rely on it in some way for their survival.

Coral reef fish are known for having beautiful, flamboyant patterns and bright colors. These patterns and colors serve several purposes, from simply identifying members of the same species to helping the fish camouflage against the coral. Their appearance might also be used to attract a mate. Certain colors can also give a warning—reds and yellows often mean that an individual has venomous spines, poisonous skin, or a sharp bite.

Finding food is a part of everyday life on the reef. With specially adapted mouths, surgeonfish and parrotfish graze on the algae that grows on the surface of coral. By removing the algae, which would otherwise smother the coral, these herbivores help to keep the reef alive. Corallivores, such as butterflyfish, consume the coral itself. They delicately pick off individual coral polyps, leaving most of the reef undamaged. These fish clear small patches on the reef where new coral can settle and grow.

Predators, such as sharks, also roam the reef, hunting for any small animals not hidden away. Small coral reef fish, like damselfish and anthias, benefit from a multitude of hiding places and safe spaces by living in this environment. The reef provides caves and tunnels that are perfect for them to hide in, away from larger fish like groupers.

While some hide, other fish openly display their presence to even the largest and most predatory of creatures, all because they provide an important service. These so-called cleaner fish remove unwanted dead scales and parasites from any fish visiting their territory. Cleaner fish receive food from the interaction, while larger animals are relieved of any itches caused by parasites.

Key to plate

1: **Longnose butterflyfish**
Forcipiger flavissimus
Length: Up to 9 inches/22 centimeters
These territorial fish use their long snout to pick tiny invertebrates out from the reefs.

2: **Mandarinfish**
Synchiropus splendidus
Length: Up to 2 inches/6 centimeters
These beautiful fish don't have scales. Instead, they have a mucus coating, which protects them from bumps and scrapes as well as parasites.

3: **Powder blue surgeonfish**
Acanthurus leucosternon
Length: Up to 9 inches/23 centimeters
Surgeonfish get their name from the sharp spine on their caudal keel (the base of their tail).

4: **Coral hind**
Cephalopholis miniata
Length: Up to 20 inches/
50 centimeters
These big fish draw food into their mouths by using a powerful suction, then swallow their prey whole.

5a: **Emperor angelfish juvenile**
5b: **Emperor angelfish adult**
Pomacanthus imperator
Length: Up to 16 inches/
40 centimeters
This angelfish looks very different as a juvenile from its adult form. It is thought that this transition prevents the adults from seeing the juveniles as a threat to space and food.

6: **Clown anemonefish**
(seen inside anemone)
Amphiprion ocellaris
Length: Up to 4 inches/11 centimeters

These fish exist in symbiosis with certain anemones found in coral reefs. Anemonefish gain protection from predators by living in the stinging tentacles of the anemone.

7a: **Bicolor parrotfish juvenile**
7b: **Bicolor parrotfish adult**
Cetoscarus bicolor
Length: Approx. 20 inches/
50 centimeters
Parrotfish are all born female, with some transforming into males later in life. Like emperor angelfish, their patterns change as they grow older.

8: **Bluestreak cleaner wrasse**
Labroides dimidiatus
Length: Approx. 4 inches/
10 centimeters
These helpful fish inhabit specific sites on a coral reef and clean any fish that come to their station.

Seahorses and Pipefish

Despite their unusual appearance and misleading name, seahorses are in fact fish. They breathe via gills and contain a swim bladder, among other fishlike features, but they also have a neck and a bony plate that covers their body and eyes.

In shallow habitats such as seagrass beds or coral reefs, seahorses use their curled, prehensile (gripping) tail to hold on tightly to things in their habitat. They are poor swimmers and would otherwise drift away from safety with the strong ocean currents. All seahorses swim using small fins on their back (dorsal fins) and steer with fins on the sides of their head (pectoral fins). Even though their dorsal fin beats thirty to seventy times a second, most seahorses reach speeds of only a few feet/meters an hour.

Although slow-paced, seahorses are remarkable hunters and successfully catch their prey of copepods (a type of zooplankton—see page 12) 90 percent of the time. By comparison, lions achieve a kill only around 20 percent of the time. Seahorses have a unique, streamlined shape to their head, which barely disturbs the water around them. It allows seahorses to sneak up on their prey unnoticed. When close enough, the seahorse will use rapid suction to catch its prey and disintegrate the food. This is important because seahorses have no teeth and so cannot chew—their food must be broken up quickly to digest.

Unlike most other animals, it is the male seahorse that gives birth. The female will make the eggs, then pass them to the male to hold in his brood pouch for incubation. The male will then look after the eggs until they hatch, expelling them in a cloud of tiny babies, known as fry, after ten to twenty-five days. In the meantime, the female seahorse will have made more eggs, ready to repeat the process. Because of the synchronization needed for seahorses to breed, a pair will stay together for at least a season, meeting every morning to hold tails and "dance" to confirm their bond.

Key to plate

1: Ornate ghost pipefish
Solenostomus paradoxus
Length: Up to 5 inches/12 centimeters
Pipefish are related to seahorses and have a straightened body and tail. Unlike others in this group, the females of this species brood and give birth to their young.

2: Long-snouted seahorse
Hippocampus guttulatus
Length: Up to 6 inches/
15 centimeters
The spiny-looking protrusions on this seahorse give it a distinctive look.

3: Leafy seadragon
Phycodurus eques
Length: 14 inches/35 centimeters
The amazing leaflike structures on the body of this Australian seahorse are purely for camouflage. They make it difficult to distinguish the seahorse from leafy seaweed fronds.

4: Big-belly seahorse
Hippocampus abdominalis
Length: Up to 14 inches/
35 centimeters
One of the biggest seahorses in the world, this species gets its name from its larger than usual abdomen. The males have larger bellies because of their brood pouch.

5: Bargibant's pygmy seahorse
Hippocampus bargibanti
Length: Up to 1 inch/2.4 centimeters
These tiny seahorses are so well camouflaged in their coral habitat that they were found only when a piece of sea fan was examined in a lab by the marine biologist Georges Bargibant in 1969.

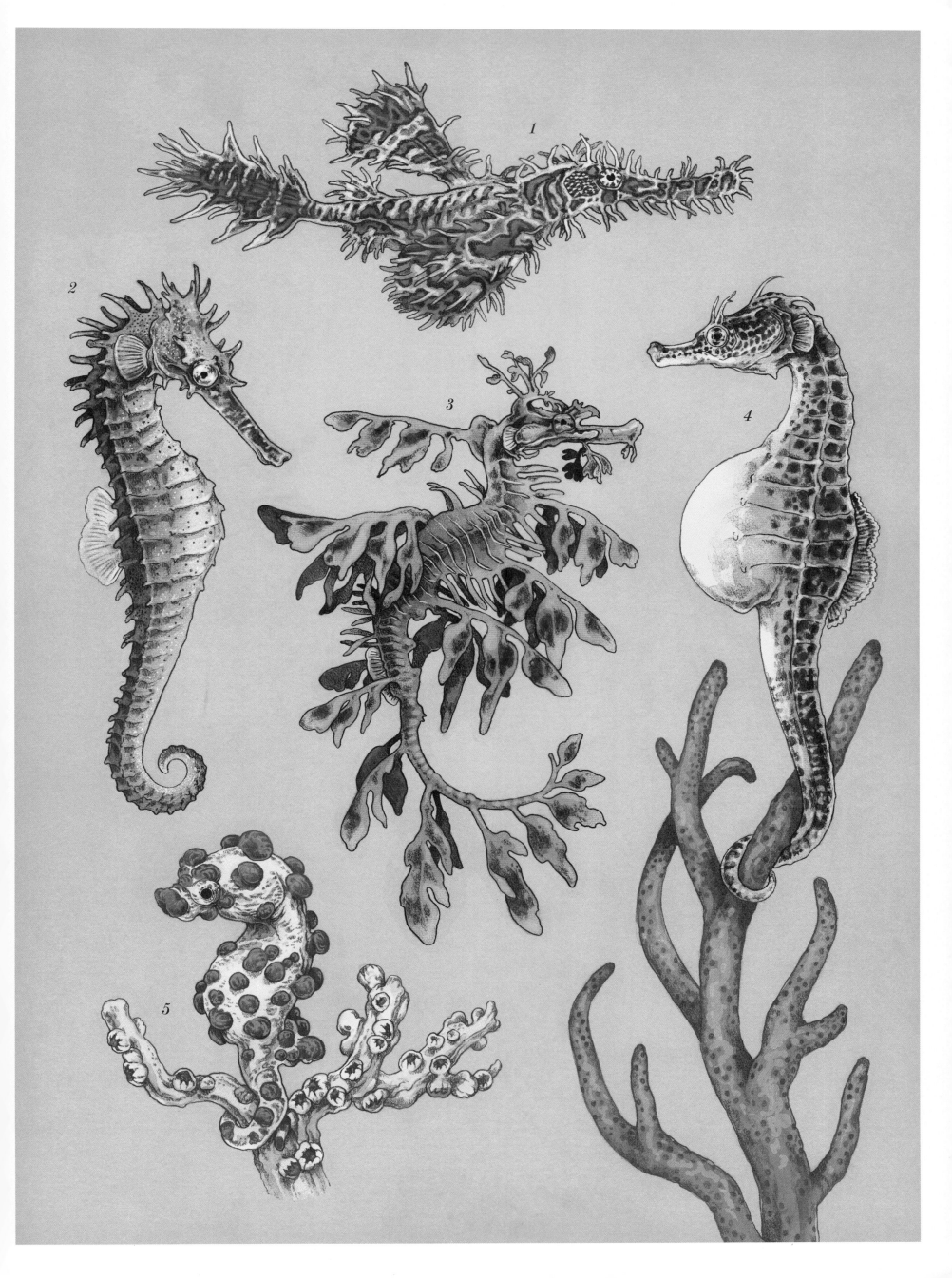

Rays and Skates

In an evolutionary history stretching back over 250 million years, there have been five cataclysmic events on earth resulting in the mass extinction of many animals—including the dinosaurs—since cartilaginous fish first appeared. This lucky group managed to evade extinction by retreating to the depths of the ocean, where they remain today.

Gracefully gliding through the water or resting undetected on the seafloor, rays and their cousins, skates, have a skeleton made of cartilage (tough, flexible tissue). Most adopt a bottom-dwelling lifestyle, feeding on shrimp and crabs, while others, like the giant manta ray, are filter feeders, "flying" through the water using winglike appendages and scooping plankton into their mouths as they go.

Over millions of years of evolution, both rays and skates have adapted highly effective ways of staying safe. From spots and speckles to marbled tones, both have sophisticated markings and patterns on their skin, making them almost undetectable against the sand below or sunlit waters above. Rays and skates often look similar, and it can be difficult to tell the difference. The stinger, or lack of one, is a differentiating feature to look for—rays have a stinger on their tail, while skates have a thicker tail, often with a small fin. Rays use their stinger to defend themselves, although they typically prefer to stay still and camouflage to avoid danger. Skates have thorny spines on their back and will usually cover themselves in sand to evade detection.

Reproduction is an interesting feature in rays and skates, and there are a variety of ways they breed. Skates encase their developing young in a tough case known as a mermaid's purse, which is laid on the seabed. The fetus will develop inside this capsule for up to a year, emerging when ready to live on its own. The mermaid's purses are disguised to look like pieces of seaweed and will eventually be covered by a film of algae, helping them to stay hidden. By comparison, rays give birth to their young fully formed, at which point they swim away to start their lives independent from their parents.

Key to plate

1: **Spotted eagle ray**
Aetobatus narinari
Width: Up to 10 feet/3 meters
Extending up to 16 feet/5 meters, much of the length of this big species is made up by its long, thin tail, which it uses to sense movement behind it.

2: **Bowmouth guitarfish**
Rhina ancylostoma
Length: Up to 10 feet/3 meters
The unmistakable body shape of this fish is between that of a shark and ray, hence its other common name of shark ray.

3: **Giant oceanic manta ray**
Mobula birostris
Width: Up to 15 feet/4.5 meters

These are the largest known rays in the world, reaching up to 23 feet/7 meters in width.

4: **Marbled electric ray**
Torpedo marmorata
Length: Up to 24 inches/60 centimeters
This ray uses its electrical charge defensively and can deliver up to 200 volts of electricity in one hit—greater voltage than that of an electric lawnmower.

5: **Knifetooth sawfish**
Anoxypristis cuspidata
Length: Up to 11½ feet/3.5 meters
Sawfish all have a long, tooth-edged nose (rostrum), which has pores for

detecting electrical fields. The sawfish can use this to find hidden prey, who give off electrical impulses.

6: **Bluespotted ribbontail ray**
Taeniura lymma
Width: Up to 14 inches/35 centimeters
The bright blue spots on this beautiful ray are attractive but warn of a dangerous sting.

7: **Undulate ray**
Raja undulata
Length: Up to 3 feet/1 meter
Despite its name, this is a species of skate. It gets its name from the undulating motion it creates with its wings while swimming.

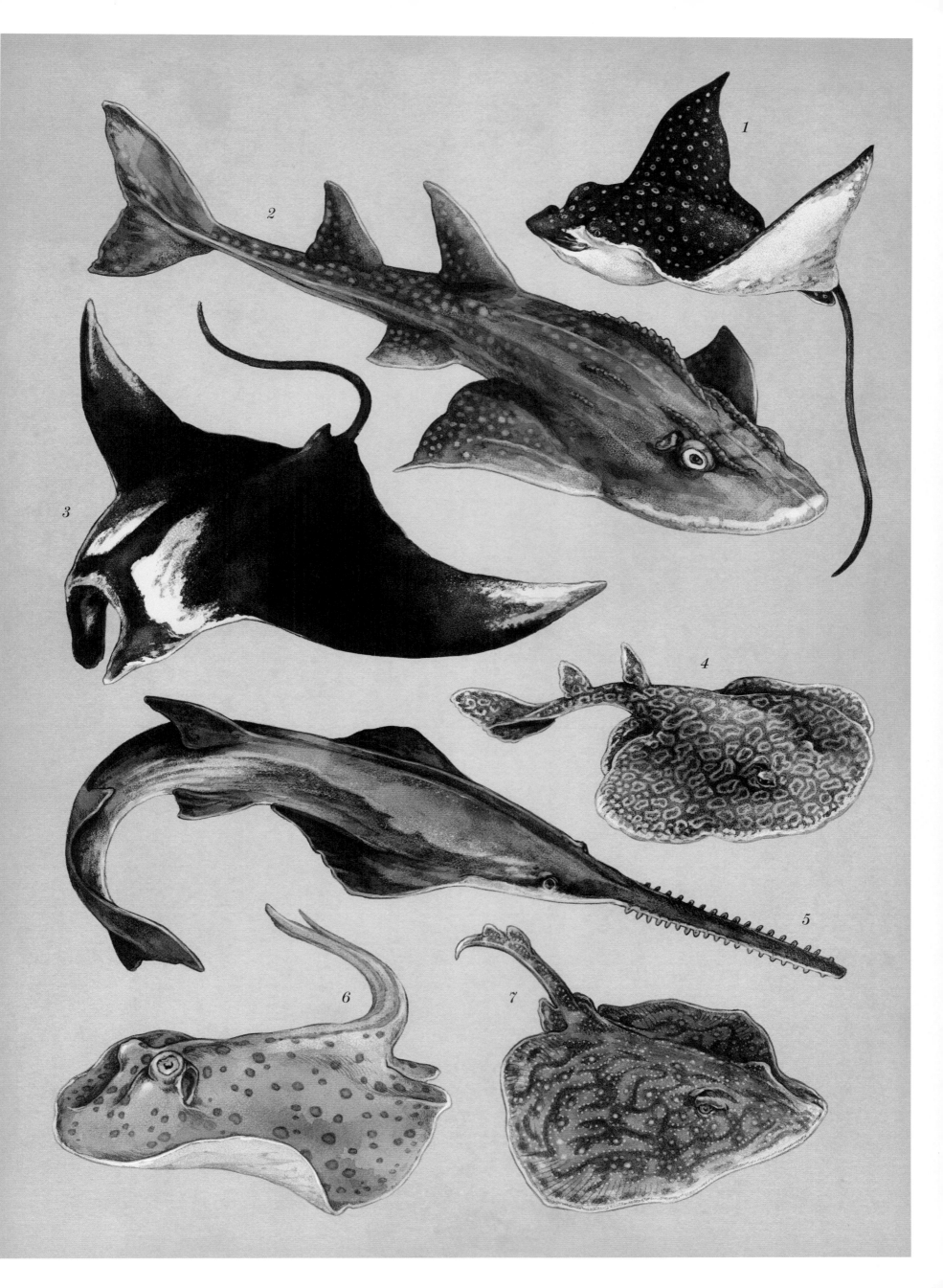

Sharks

These prehistoric animals have roamed the ocean for around 450 million years, and today there more than five hundred species of shark. Although sharks are much maligned and often feared by humans, the truth is that only a handful of species are responsible for bites, and attacks are incredibly rare. These fascinating animals have evolved to be hugely varied in size, shape, and lifestyle, and it is because of these many adaptations that they have maintained their position as the ocean's top predator.

With an enormous habitat to hunt in, sharks must use their senses to track down a meal over huge distances. Along with their incredible sense of smell, sight, touch, taste, and hearing, these highly perceptive creatures have an extra sense that allows them to detect the electricity produced by the muscle movement of living things. They do this via tiny, jelly-filled pores that are dotted around the head, particularly on the underside of the snout. Named after the Italian scientist who discovered them, these electroreceptors, known as ampullae of Lorenzini, are able to detect very low charges in water—great white sharks can detect one millionth of a volt.

Efficiency is important when traveling such vast distances, too. Sharks have special streamlining scales known as dermal denticles. These scales are shaped like teeth and all point the same way, from nose to tail. This arrangement helps to reduce drag and turbulence, which lets the sharks cut through water easily, allowing for faster and quieter swimming. Sharks also have a superlight cartilage skeleton, which provides extra speed. The only bony part of a shark is their teeth, which have evolved to be unique to each species and perfectly suited to their prey. They form in multiple rows in a shark's mouth and will constantly regrow throughout their lives.

As well as being impressive and beautiful creatures, sharks are incredibly important to the health of our ocean, too. Sharks tend to hunt for animals that are sick and therefore easier to catch. Without sharks, disease would spread more easily.

Key to plate

1: **Epaulette shark**
Hemiscyllium ocellatum
Length: Up to 35 inches/
90 centimeters
These small sharks will often use their pectoral and pelvic fins to walk on the seabed, rather than swim.

2: **Great white shark**
Carcharodon carcharias
Length: Approx. 16 feet/5 meters
This revered animal can keep its blood temperature up to 14°F/8°C higher than the surrounding water.

3: **Common thresher shark**
Alopias vulpinus
Length: Approx. 16 feet/5 meters
The extra-long upper lobe of the caudal fin (tail) is used to stun fish.

4: **Cookiecutter shark**
Isistius brasiliensis
Length: Up to 22 inches/
56 centimeters
This small shark is parasitic, attaching itself to larger animals to bite off chunks of flesh. The deep bite marks are perfectly rounded, giving this shark its name.

5: **Basking shark**
Cetorhinus maximus
Length: Approx. 26 feet/8 meters
Second only in size to the whale shark, these enormous fish are in fact plankton eaters.

6: **Tasselled wobbegong**
Eucrossorhinus dasypogon
Length: Up to 4 feet/1.25 meters

This incredible camouflaged shark has a fringe of dermal lobes that make it look like coral or algae to an unsuspecting fish. This, along with their complex patterns, makes them masters of disguise.

7: **Oceanic whitetip shark**
Carcharhinus longimanus
Length: Approx. 10 feet/3 meters
These sharks are named for their large, rounded fins with white tips.

Whale Shark

Whale sharks are ocean-roaming giants, migrating huge distances to reach the richest feeding grounds. They eat microscopic plankton as well as tiny fish and eggs, filtering them from the water with their massive mouths. Reaching lengths of around 33 feet/ 10 meters, whale sharks are the largest fish in the world, yet certain aspects of their lives still remain a mystery to us.

Large groups of whale sharks are seen seasonally in the waters off the Yucatán Peninsula in Mexico. They are thought to gather here to eat the millions of eggs produced by spawning tuna. Regular sightings have led the area to become a hot spot for wildlife tourism as well as shark research. One female tagged here was documented completing a migration of around 4,350 miles/7,000 kilometers, covering about 31 miles/50 kilometers a day. It is possible that she was traveling to give birth to her young, maybe out in the open ocean.

Nobody has ever seen a whale shark give birth, so we can only guess where this takes place. Scientists think females may go to remote islands like the Galápagos and give birth deep underwater. From a specimen caught in 1996, we know that whale sharks give birth to live pups that hatch from eggs inside their mother, which is known as ovoviviparous reproduction. In this specimen, there were three hundred pups measuring 16 to 24 inches/

40 to 60 centimeters long, relatively small considering the gargantuan size of the adults.

Instead of using electronic tagging, more and more researchers are relying on a different method to identify whale sharks and record their movements. This technique is based on recognizing the unique pattern of spots found across the sides and back of all whale sharks—a pattern as unique as a human fingerprint. Using this arrangement, scientists can identify individuals from photographs and see how far a single shark has traveled without having to tag it. This used to be a long, slow process, until an algorithm to identify star constellations was adapted to work on whale shark spots. Now computer software can aid with the identification of individual whale sharks, helping us to learn more about the lives of these incredible animals.

Key to plate

1: **Whale shark**
Rhincodon typus
Length: Up to 33 feet/10 meters
This animal is named for its large size and for its filter-feeding behavior, which it has in common with baleen whales. Whale sharks live in open, tropical waters around the world. Although nobody can be sure, they are thought to grow up to 33 feet/ 10 meters long and can live to be more than 100 years old, beginning to

reach sexual maturity at around 30 years old.

2: **Golden trevally pilotfish**
Gnathanodon speciosus
Length: Up to 4 feet/1.2 meters
These brightly colored pilot fish are often found alongside whale sharks. They are attracted by the leftover food the whale shark leaves behind when it is feeding.

3: **Remora**
Remora remora
Length: Approx. 16 inches/ 40 centimeters
Remora fish suction on to larger animals such as whale sharks and use them to hitch a ride over long distances. The whale shark is not affected positively or negatively by this.

Habitat: Mangrove Forest

Mangrove trees can survive conditions that would kill most other plants. Growing in tropical coastal areas, these resilient plants can withstand salty water, intense sunshine, changing tides, and crashing waves. This is thanks to a number of unique adaptations: prop roots branch from the trunk and strengthen trees, which enables them to withstand storms; porous upright roots take in oxygen from the air, replenishing low oxygen levels in the silty water; and leaves can filter out as much as 90 percent of the salt from the water their roots absorb.

Where roots enter the water, they create caves and tunnels—the perfect hiding places for fish and other small animals. This is especially useful for young animals, including lemon shark pups, which may use the mangrove as a nursery before starting their adult lives in other habitats. Other creatures live in the mangroves for their whole lives or will come and go seasonally. Specialized animals, such as the mudskipper, even take advantage of the living space above the water, hopping and sliding on the mud to catch a meal of insects.

Because mangrove trees grow along coastlines, they offer excellent natural protection from erosion. Without mangroves, coastal communities would experience more frequent damage from storms that blow in from the ocean. Mangrove forests are also incredibly important for the role they play in sheltering young fish. These juveniles later go on to support food chains across the ocean, providing food for thousands of different animals—including humans.

Key to plate

Mangrove forest, Southeast Asia

1: **Fiddler crab**
Uca annulipes
Carapace width: Up to 4/5 inch/
2 centimeters
Males have one small claw and one large one, which they wave in the air to attract a female.

2: **Mangrove plant**
Rhizophora racemosa
Height: Approx. 98 feet/30 meters
Rhizophora seeds can survive floating in water for days or weeks until they reach a good site to grow.

3: **Barred mudskipper**
Periophthalmus argentilineatus
Length: Up to 7½ inches/
19 centimeters

Mudskippers can survive out of the water when the mangrove's tides drop each day.

4: **Hardyhead silverside**
Atherinomorus lacunosus
Length: Approx. 5 inches/
12 centimeters>
Shoals of these little fish can contain several hundred individuals.

5: **Indo-Pacific tarpon**
Megalops cyprinoides
Length: Up to 59 inches/
45.5 centimeters
The tarpon uses its swim bladder to breathe air, taking in more oxygen, which gives it short bursts of energy.

6: **Sicklefin lemon shark**
Negaprion acutidens
Length: Up to 12½ feet/3.8 meters
When these sharks are pups, they shelter and hunt in the mangrove.

7: **Silver moony**
Monodactylus argenteus
Length: Approx. 5 inches/
12 centimeters
Stripes make it hard for other animals to tell which way the moony is facing.

8: Rhizophora racemosa **seed**
Length: Up to 12 inches/
30 centimeters
When ready, these seeds drop into the water and are carried away by currents. Once in a suitable location, they settle and grow.

Gallery 6

Mammals

Cetaceans
Blue Whale
Pinnipeds
Manatees and Dugongs
Habitat: Kelp Forest

Cetaceans

Found throughout the ocean from the tropics to the freezing poles, cetaceans are a group of marine mammals that include whales, dolphins, and porpoises. All members of this enigmatic group share special adaptations that allow them to swim enormous distances and stay warm.

Cetaceans have many of the same features as land mammals—they are warm-blooded, breathe air with their lungs, and care for their young, feeding them highly nutritious milk. Like their mammal cousins on land, this group also has some hair, mostly in the form of sensory whiskers around the mouth. Yet despite their similarities with land mammals, cetaceans have very different ways of feeding. The odontocetes, or toothed whales, have small, sharp teeth suited to hunting and killing large prey, while the mysticetes—baleen whales—use brush-like baleen to filter tiny plankton from the water. As animals that breathe air, cetaceans also need to hold their breath to hunt for prey. Sperm whales dive to depths of around 7,380 feet/2,250 meters and can hold their breath for up to 90 minutes.

Cetaceans often feed and breed in different parts of the ocean, and they must travel between the two areas every year. As strong, powerful swimmers, and with a thick layer of fatty blubber for insulation, they are well-equipped for these voyages. The migratory journeys can cover huge distances, with some species repeating yearly migrations of nearly 3,100 miles/5,000 kilometers. Incredibly, humpback whales are known to complete a 10,200-mile/16,400-kilometer round trip, traveling between the equator and Antarctica.

These long-distance ocean migrants need to communicate with others of their species to survive, and they do this in sophisticated and surprising ways. Baleen whales use deep-sounding songs that travel huge distances, while dolphins communicate via clicks and whistles. Regional groups of whales and dolphins can even have dialects and individual sounds for each other, a bit like human voices.

Key to plate

1: **Short-beaked common dolphin**
Delphinus delphis
Length: Up to 8 feet/2.5 meters
Found in groups of hundreds, if not thousands, of individuals, these animals are very social and spend all their time together.

2: **Commerson's dolphin**
Cephalorhynchus commersonii
Length: Up to 6 feet/1.8 meters
These small dolphins are playful and agile swimmers, often swimming upside down or leaping into the air.

3: **Sperm whale**
Physeter macrocephalus

Length: Up to 59 feet/18 meters
This deep-sea diver is known to prey on giant squid.

4: **Harbor porpoise**
Phocoena phocoena
Length: Up to 6½ feet/2 meters
Porpoises are very similar in appearance to dolphins but have a shorter beak with flatter, spade-shaped teeth.

5: **Humpback whale**
Megaptera novaeangliae
Length: Up to 52 feet/16 meters
Despite their name, these whales do not have a hump on their back, but

they form a distinctive curved shape when diving underwater.

6: **Common minke whale**
Balaenoptera acutorostrata
Length: Approx. 35 feet/10.7 meters
One of the smallest baleen whales, this species is often preyed upon by orcas (see page 74).

7: **Beluga whale**
Delphinapterus leucas
Length: Up to 16 feet/5 meters
Like all polar whales, the beluga has no dorsal fin. This means it can swim beneath the ice without scraping itself.

MAMMALS

Blue Whale

The blue whale is the largest animal that has ever lived on our planet, reaching lengths of up to 98 feet/30 meters. Weighing almost 220 tons/200 metric tons, blue whales can have a heart the size of a small car. Their enormous size surpasses that of the largest dinosaurs and is only possible because blue whales live in water—a supportive environment that prevents their weight from crushing their organs. These leviathans have been cruising our ocean for nearly 1.5 million years, but during the twentieth century, whales were hunted extensively for their meat, oil, and bones. The blue whale population dropped by more than 99 percent. Faced with extinction, blue whales were protected from commercial whaling by the International Convention for the Regulation of Whaling in 1966 and have slowly started to recover. Despite this, their population today is still at a fraction of the pre-commercial whaling numbers.

In addition to being the largest, blue whales are also one of the loudest animals in the world. Males are the most vocal and can reach 188 decibels—louder than a jet engine. Although their songs can be detected by other blue whales hundreds of miles/kilometers away, they cannot be heard by humans because their low-pitched frequency is too deep for us to hear.

Interestingly, the largest animal on earth survives by eating one of the smallest.

Shoals of tiny krill are sieved from the ocean by these giants using baleen—plates of hairlike fibers that hang in their mouth. Blue whales can eat around 4½ tons/4 metric tons of krill in a single day with an enormous mouth that expands via pleats in their throat. In a feeding lunge, blue whales engulf not only thousands of individual krill but also tons of water. Their huge baleen plates catch and sieve out the food to be swallowed down a relatively small throat.

Blue whales migrate between cold and warm waters, spending the warmer months feeding at the poles and the cooler months nearer the equator where they meet to breed. Females have babies every two to three years and are pregnant for around a year before giving birth to a calf more than 23 feet/7 meters long.

———————————————— *Key to plate* ————————————————

1: **Blue whale**
Balaenoptera musculus
Length: Up to 98 feet/30 meters
Blue whales need large quantities of food from reliable sources. As they migrate from their breeding to feeding grounds, they must remember where their prey are most plentiful. Scientists think that blue whales use

their memory from past journeys to return to the best spots and time their migrations to when there is the most krill to eat.

2: **Calf**
Length: Approx. 23 feet/7 meters at birth
A baby will feed on about

53 gallons/200 liters of its mother's rich, fatty milk, gaining weight at a rate of 220 pounds/100 kilograms a day. It will gradually stop feeding when it is six months old, by which time it will be around 52 feet/16 meters long.

Pinnipeds

The pinnipeds are a group that includes some of the fastest and most agile marine mammals, most of which survive in the coldest waters on earth. These sleek predators are most at home swimming underwater, but they also make use of land or ice floes as a refuge from predators. There are three subgroups within the pinnipeds: seals, sea lions, and walruses.

True seals are identifiable by their lack of visible ears. Perfectly adapted for life in glacial water, seals have large eyes that work well in the dark and a thick coat of blubber and fur that keeps them warm and further streamlines their bodies. Seals usually breed on solid ground or on ice floes around the Arctic or Antarctica, but are not well-adapted for life on land, as they can't use their back flippers out of the water. Instead, they must use their strong stomach muscles and short front flippers to pull themselves forward.

Sea lions and the closely related fur seals do have visible ear flaps on the sides of their head. They are agile, graceful swimmers and can twist and turn in the water much more easily than seals. They often spend time out of the water and can rotate their long muscular flippers forward to walk on land.

The third subgroup of pinnipeds has only one species: the walrus. Formidable in appearance, these hefty creatures spend a lot of their lives in water, hunting for clams and other invertebrates. Once they find a meal, walruses use their lips to clamp over it and pull their tongue backward, causing enough suction to pull the animal from its shell. Other than its size, the main defining feature of the walrus is their enormous tusks, which both males and females possess. These nearly 3-feet-/1-meter-long teeth are used by males to display dominance and win the right to breed with females, but they are also used to keep ice holes open in the winter—vital for any air-breathing mammal living on the ice.

Key to plate

1: **Ribbon seal with pup**
Histriophoca fasciata
Length: Up to 6 feet/1.9 meters
The striking patterns of the ribbon seal develop as they grow. These seals are born white and later molt, looking like their parents at around 3 years old.

2: **Antarctic fur seal**
Arctocephalus gazella
Length: Up to 6 feet/1.8 meters
The fur of these creatures was so popular as clothing in the eighteenth and nineteenth centuries they were hunted almost to extinction.

3: **Californian sea lion**
Zalophus californianus
Length: Up to 8 feet/2.4 meters
Like all pinnipeds, sea lions have vibrissae (whiskers) around their face, which help them to detect the movements of prey in the water.

4: **Walrus**
Odobenus rosmarus
Length: 7½–12 feet/2.3–3.6 meters
Weighing over 3,300 pounds/1,500 kilograms, these adults may eat as many as 6,000 clams in one feeding season.

5: **Harbor seal**
Phoca vitulina
Length: Up to 6 feet/1.9 meters
Harbor seals live in the Northern Hemisphere, where they feed on crustaceans, mollusks, and fish.

6: **Southern elephant seal**
Mirounga leonine
Length: 8½–19 feet/2.6–5.8 meters
One of the deepest diving mammals, this species has been recorded at depths of over 6,500 feet/2,000 meters. The males have protruding noses, which they use to attract females.

Manatees and Dugongs

Gracefully swimming in shallow waters, these marine mammals were once mistaken for mythical creatures by sailors. They have since inspired many tales of mermaids, and the order Sirenia—to which manatees and dugongs belong—in fact derives its name from the Greek word for "siren."

Today, manatees and dugongs are also known as sea cows. With large bodies, a slow lifestyle, and the need to graze for hours at a time, they do have similarities with their land-based namesake, and are the only herbivorous marine mammals still alive today. Their cousins, the Steller's sea cows, were hunted to extinction, and unfortunately, the populations of both manatees and dugongs are today classified as vulnerable. Although both mammals are aquatic, they still need to breathe air and resurface every five minutes or so to take a breath.

Occupying the tropical waters around the north coast of Australia, India, Indonesia, and eastern Africa, dugongs use their strong, flexible upper lip to pull up seagrass—of which they must consume up to 110 pounds/50 kilograms a day. This activity leaves furrows behind in the seabed and often disturbs small invertebrates, making an easy meal for golden trevally fish that often trail alongside the dugongs.

3

The three species of manatee are found in different locations: the Caribbean, West Africa, and the Amazon basin. Unlike dugongs, manatees can travel into rivers from the sea, and the Amazonian manatee lives exclusively in fresh water. With no insulating blubber, manatees must stay in water with temperatures above 64°F/18°C. This means they migrate in the colder months, sometimes finding warm springs in fresh water where many individuals will huddle together for warmth.

Despite having few natural predators, many manatee and dugong populations are in decline. Affected by toxic algal blooms (see page 10) and the loss of warm marine habitats, many of these animals are also killed or seriously injured in watercraft accidents every year.

Key to plate

1: Steller's sea cow skull
Hydrodamalis gigas
Length of skull: Approx. 24 inches/
61 centimeters
Hunted to extinction by 1768, all that remains today of the Steller's sea cow are fossils such as this. They reached enormous sizes, growing up to
33 feet/10 meters long and weighing as much as 12 tons/11 metric tons—larger than many modern-day whales.

2: Dugong
Dugong dugon
Length: Up to 10 feet/3 meters
Dugongs are slightly smaller than manatees and have fluked tails similar to dolphins. This is the only species of dugong alive today.

3: West Indian manatee
Trichechus manatus
Length: Up to 11½ feet/3.5 meters

Manatees are distinguishable from dugongs by their large, rounded paddle tail and nails on their flippers. The largest member of their group today, this species of manatee is increasing in numbers thanks to conservation efforts.

Habitat: Kelp Forest

Kelp is a kind of seaweed that grows in cool coastal regions. Unlike plants on land, which have roots, seaweeds have a gripping holdfast that attaches to the rocky seabed, anchoring them against storms and ocean currents. Each holdfast has one or more stipes (stalks) reaching up to the surface. Air-filled floats called pneumatocysts prevent the stipes from sinking and ensure the kelp is close enough to the sunlit surface to photosynthesize. Some types of kelp grow as tall as 148 feet/45 meters, forming vast forests that tower above the seabed. Just like a rainforest on land, this ecosystem has several layers where animals can shelter and find food: otters snooze in the canopy; sharks stalk prey in the kelp's corridors; and invertebrates shuffle slowly across the seafloor among the kelp's holdfasts.

As in all ecosystems, there is a delicate balance between photosynthesizing organisms (such as seaweed), herbivores, and carnivores. In the kelp forest, this balance is best seen in the relationship between kelp, sea urchins, and sea otters. Sea urchins graze on the kelp, making space for new plant growth. Sea otters then feed on the urchins, which controls their population and prevents overgrazing. However, sea otter hunting in the eighteenth and nineteenth centuries led to fewer otters to keep the urchins in balance. The sea urchins boomed, feasting on the kelp, which in places died back completely, creating areas known as urchin barrens. Kelp forests are susceptible to other changes, too. Frequent storms can rip the kelp from its holdfast; warming seas bring fewer nutrients needed for kelp growth; and poor water quality reduces the light levels needed for photosynthesis. As our ocean warms due to climate change, kelp forests may move farther north to cooler waters.

Key to plate

Kelp forest, Californian coast

1: Southern sea otter
Enhydra lutris nereis
Length: Up to 4½ feet/1.4 meters
Sea otters were hunted extensively for their fur in the 1700s and 1800s. Conservation efforts are helping their numbers to recover.

2: Bull kelp
Nereocystis luetkeana
Length: Up to 118 feet/36 meters
Bull kelp extracts are used in a range of everyday items, including ice cream.

3: Garibaldi fish
Hypsypops rubicundus
Length: Approx. 12 inches/30 centimeters
Territorial males defend a nest site year-round. In the spring, a male will clean the nest site and entice females with swimming performances.

4: Leopard shark
Triakis semifasciata
Length: Approx. 5 feet/1.6 meters
Young sharks are experts at finding snails and crabs under the sandy seabed and often frequent kelp forests.

5: Giant kelp
Macrocystis pyrifera
Length: Approx. 148 feet/45 meters
Giant kelp can grow as much as 18 inches/45 centimeters a day, making it one of the fastest-growing organisms on earth. When detached from the seabed, it floats in mats, giving shelter to many animals.

6: California sheephead
Semicossyphus pulcher
Length: Approx. 36 inches/91 centimeters
This species starts out as a female and turns into a male later in life.

7: Purple sea urchin
Strongylocentrotus purpuratus
Length: Up to 4 inches/10 centimeters
These voracious invertebrates pose a threat to kelp forests—90 percent of the bull kelp forests in California have been devoured by them.

8: Rockfish
Sebastes sp.
Length: 5–41 inches/12–104 centimeters, depending on species
Some of the longest-lived fish, rockfish may live for 100 years or more.

Gallery 7

Birds

Seabirds
Habitat: The Poles

Seabirds

Seabirds make up about 3.5 percent of all bird species. Whether they spend the majority of their lives gliding over the waves like the wandering albatross or visit the ocean only to collect food like the puffin, these birds all have a connection to the water. Their plumage is often less colorful than that of other birds, which helps them camouflage against the ocean waves.

The hunting methods of seabirds vary with each species. Some, like the blue-footed booby, will dive almost 98 feet/30 meters from the air into the ocean in pursuit of prey. Others are better adapted to surface feeding, either skimming the water while still in flight or, in the case of the Wilson's storm petrel, stopping for a moment to dip their feet in the water, which attracts plankton to the water's surface. Penguins have given up flight altogether and have strong, short wings that behave more like flippers, providing powerful swimming strokes underwater.

Many seabirds migrate to breed, with some traveling enormous distances. Wandering albatross have been known to fly around 10,000 miles/16,100 kilometers in a single journey, barely flapping their wings. Instead, they use the wind, catching updrafts to keep themselves airborne and to conserve energy. Each season, they gather on rocky outcrops in the ocean or on cliffs. Males and females pair up, with some returning to each other after long periods apart. This bonding between parents allows them to successfully care for their chick while one adult is away foraging for food.

Such a strategy is important for emperor penguins, too—the only animal that spends the winter in Antarctica. These amazing birds will walk 50 to 75 miles/80 to 120 kilometers inland to breed in colonies. Once the egg is laid and hatched, the pair will take turns guarding their chick while the other returns to feed at sea. Only by working together can they raise the next generation of emperor penguins in such extreme conditions.

Key to plate

1: **Herring gull**
Larus argentatus
Wingspan: Up to 5 feet/1.5 meters
These opportunistic birds will scavenge food from waste and even take it directly from people.

2: **Wilson's storm petrel**
Oceanites oceanicus
Wingspan: Up to 16½ inches/
42 centimeters
At home in stormy seas, these birds fly through the troughs of the waves, avoiding the worst of the weather.

3: **Red-billed tropicbird**
Phaethon aethereus
Wingspan: Up to 4½ feet/1.4 meters
A favorite food for this bird is flying fish, which they are known to catch midair.

4: **Wandering albatross**
Diomedea exulans

Wingspan: Up to 11½ feet/3.5 meters
Wandering albatrosses have the largest wingspan of any bird and can spend years at sea without returning to land once.

5: **Blue-footed booby**
Sula nebouxii
Wingspan: Up to 5 feet/1.5 meters
The bright blue feet on these birds are used by the males to attract a mate as part of a display of courtship.

6: **Atlantic puffin**
Fratercula arctica
Wingspan: Up to 25 inches/
63 centimeters
When the breeding season is finished, these birds shed their colorful beak plates and eye patches.

7: **Australian pelican**
Pelecanus conspicillatus
Wingspan: Up to 8 feet/2.5 meters

This species has the longest beak of any known bird, reaching just under 2 feet/52 centimeters.

8: **Emperor penguin**
Aptenodytes forsteri
Height: Up to 4 feet/1.2 meters
This is the largest penguin species. They can dive to depths of 1,640 feet/ 500 meters in search of food.

9: **African penguin**
Spheniscus demersus
Height: Up to 28 inches/
70 centimeters
The only penguin to be found on the continent of Africa, this penguin has to cope with hotter environments than those of its cousins in colder climates. The pink patch above their eye helps them to lose heat.

Habitat: The Poles

Some of the most extreme environments on earth are found at the North and South Poles. Almost inhospitable, with temperatures as low as −112°F/−80°C, winds that reach 100 miles/160 kilometers an hour, and darkness for half the year, these ice-covered regions of the world are home to only the toughest creatures.

Antarctica is a continent found at the southernmost tip of our planet and is covered in and surrounded by ice. The Arctic is an area of ocean at the northernmost reaches of earth and forms part of several countries, including Finland, Norway, Denmark, Iceland, Greenland, Russia, Canada, and the United States. The polar regions are diverse, with some areas experiencing seasonal melts and some covered permanently in ice up to 10 feet/3 meters thick. The soil on land, known as tundra, is permanently frozen and supports only low-growing plants with shallow roots.

First impressions might suggest that it would be difficult for life to thrive here, yet the Arctic is home to many animals, from mystical-looking narwhals to majestic polar bears and a host of migratory seabirds and marine life. Such a diverse range of wildlife can be found here because, in part, the cold waters are nutrient-rich, providing the perfect conditions for phytoplankton to bloom. These important microscopic creatures are the first link in the food chain, which includes top predators like polar bears and orcas.

As the seasons change and temperatures vary, the fluctuating levels of ice can influence the life cycles of the wildlife. Humpback whales, for example, swim from their breeding grounds in warm, tropical waters to the Arctic or Antarctica during the summer to access water usually trapped under ice during the winter. But scientific evidence shows that sea ice is melting unusually fast due to climate change, altering the habits of these creatures.

The ice in our polar regions has a wider effect on our planet, too. In what is known as the albedo effect, the bright white ice reflects light and heat back into space, keeping Earth cool and the climate constant. Without polar ice, more of the sun's heat will become trapped and our planet will get much hotter. It is vital that we monitor and reduce our impact on these vulnerable parts of the world, or we could be faced with an ice-free Arctic in the near future.

Key to plate

Arctic ice shelf, Arctic Ocean

1: **Arctic tern**
Sterna paradisaea
Wingspan: Up to 30 inches/
75 centimeters
These birds migrate incredible distances, flying between the Arctic and Antarctica, to catch the summer season in both. They travel around 22,000 miles/35,000 kilometers each year.

2: **Polar bear**
Ursus maritimus ·
Length: Up to 10 feet/3 meters

The biggest bear in the world and the largest land carnivore, the polar bear spends most of its time on the Arctic sea ice. It is also a strong swimmer.

3: **Narwhal**
Monodon monoceros
Length: Up to 18 feet/5.5 meters
Male narwhals have spiral-shaped horns that can reach up to 10 feet/3 meters in length.

4: **Arctic cod**
Arctogadus glacialis
Length: Approx. 13 inches/
32.5 centimeters

Amazingly, Arctic cod have a kind of antifreeze in their blood. This stops them from freezing in the icy waters around the poles.

5: **Orca**
Orcinus orca
Length: Up to 26 feet/8 meters
These apex predators can communicate to hunt together and are one of the most intelligent cetaceans known (see page 60).

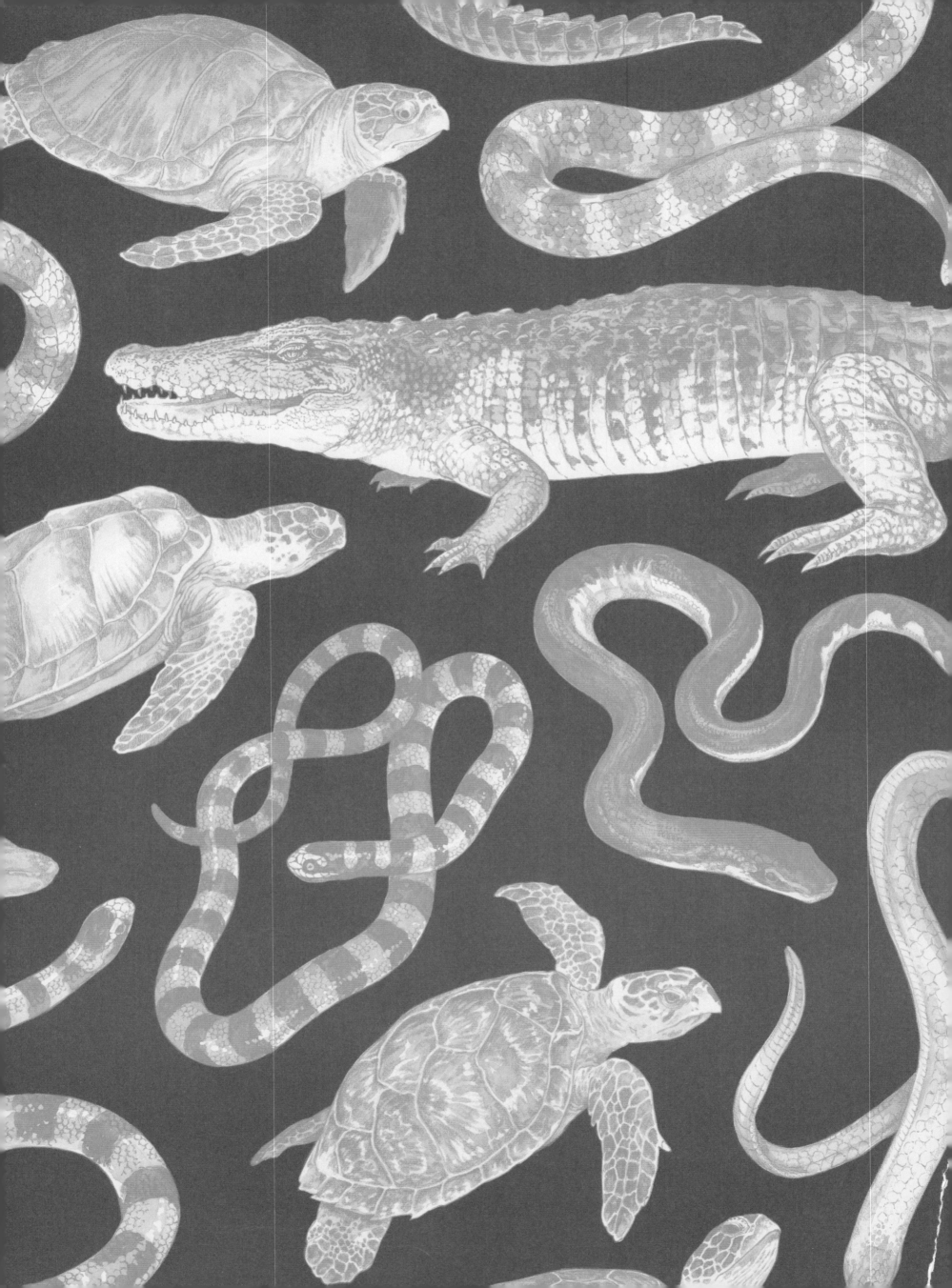

Gallery 8

Reptiles

Turtles
Saltwater Crocodile
Sea Snakes
Habitat: Galápagos Islands

Turtles

Sea turtles are ancient creatures that have lived in the ocean for around 200 million years, making them one of the oldest reptiles alive today. With their thick protective shells, streamlined bodies, and powerful webbed flippers, they are well-adapted for life at sea. Often completing journeys of thousands of miles across entire oceans, they are strong swimmers with an amazing ability to navigate through featureless expanses of open water.

Sea turtles have varied diets that differ between species. Loggerhead turtles are omnivorous, eating a range of crustaceans, mollusks, and coral, as well as algae. Other turtles are more selective. The leatherback, for example, has a diet that consists mainly of jellyfish. Green turtles change their diet as they grow, with omnivorous juveniles becoming mostly herbivorous adults. The algae and seagrass consumed by the adult green turtles turn their flesh and fat green, which gives this species its name.

When not sleeping, eating, or mating, turtles migrate between feeding and breeding areas. Leatherback turtles have been known to travel 10,000 miles/16,000 kilometers in search of jellyfish to eat. Some loggerhead turtles swim nearly 8,000 miles/13,000 kilometers from Japan to Mexico to feed, then return to Japan to breed—a round trip of 16,000 miles/26,000 kilometers.

Much as humans use satellite navigation, turtles use the planet's magnetic field to find the beach on which they were hatched, returning every season to lay their own eggs. This incredible journey is followed by the enormous physical challenge of dragging their heavy bodies out of the water, digging a large hole, and laying their eggs—around one hundred in a single nest. After covering the nest, the females return to the ocean, leaving the eggs to incubate beneath the sand. Young turtles are a great source of nutrition, and many predators eagerly wait for them to hatch. As a defense mechanism, the babies will all emerge at the same time and race down the beach toward the sea. Once in the ocean, they will spend their whole life in the water, with females only leaving to lay their own eggs, returning to the same beach.

Key to plate

1: Loggerhead turtle
Caretta caretta
Shell length: Approx. 4 feet/
1.2 meters
Named for its large head and strong jaws, these turtles are able to crush clamshells and crunch sea urchins.

2: Hawksbill turtle
Eretmochelys imbricata
Shell length: Up to 35 inches/
90 centimeters
This species' shell is unique in that its shell sections (scutes) overlap, creating a beautiful, distinctive pattern.

3: Leatherback turtle
Dermochelys coriacea
Shell length: Up to 7 feet/2.2 meters
Weighing around 1,000 pounds/
500 kilograms, leatherback turtles are the largest living sea turtles. Unlike other turtles, they can swim in colder waters.

4: Olive ridley turtle
Lepidochelys olivacea
Shell length: Up to 24 inches/
60 centimeters
The most abundant of all the species, this small turtle nests in huge numbers in an event called an arribada.

5: Green turtle
Chelonia mydas
Shell length: Approx. 3½ feet/
1.1 meters
Of all the sea turtle species, green turtles are the only herbivorous adults. They are also the only sea turtles to leave the water for purposes other than laying eggs—they sunbathe on beaches to keep warm.

Saltwater Crocodile

Saltwater crocodiles are the biggest living reptiles in the world and have a lineage that stretches back to the time of the dinosaurs. With massive, powerful bodies, including a formidable set of jaws and a long muscular tail, these creatures are capable of ambushing large prey such as zebras, buffalo, and even sharks. They are often found in estuaries where the river meets the ocean.

These enormous predators lurk beneath the surface, barely visible to unsuspecting prey coming to drink at the water's edge. They attack with spectacular speed and agility, holding on tightly with a jaw strength more powerful than any other animal on Earth and dragging their prey underwater. At this point, the crocodile will roll, in a technique known as the death roll, causing its victim to drown. But their eating habits are not always so violent. Saltwalter crocodiles are unfussy eaters; they will also eat a variety of smaller creatures from the shallow waters and shores where they live, including crabs, snails, and fish.

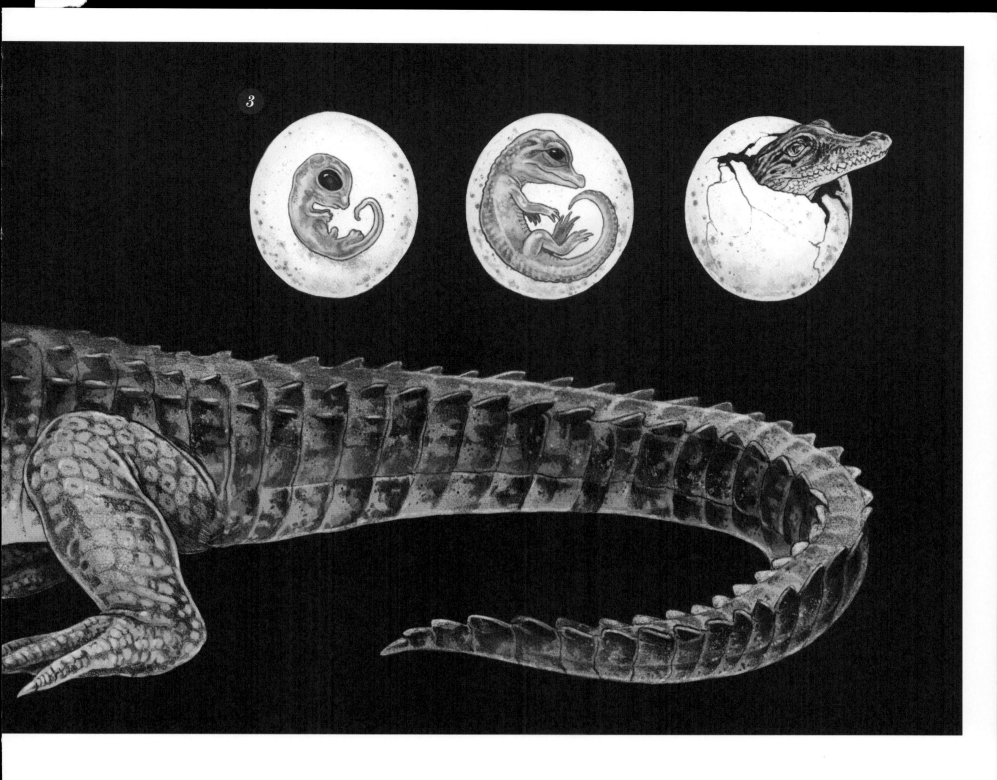

Despite their fearsome reputation, female saltwater crocodiles are attentive and caring parents. Mothers lay their eggs in piles of mud and vegetation and continually guard and tend to them. The sex of the babies is decided by the temperature at which they develop—lower temperatures produce females and higher temperatures produce males. After an incubation period of a few months, the hatchlings will call to their mother, who will dig them out of the nest and gently carry them in her mouth to the water where she will care for them for several months.

──────────────── *Key to plate* ────────────────

1: **Saltwater crocodile**
Crocodylus porosus
Length: Up to 11½ feet/3.5 meters
(females), 17 feet/5.2 meters (males)
Because these impressive reptiles
rely on fresh water and land to live
and breed, they aren't thought of
as marine reptiles, and often only
travel through the ocean to get to a
new island. Scientists think they use
ocean currents to "surf" on, instead of
paddling with their webbed feet.

2: **Crocodile eye**
Crocodiles can focus horizontally
across their field of vision. This means
that they can search for prey on the
shore without moving their head. Their
eyes and nostrils are located on the
top of their head so they can almost
fully submerge while still being able to
keep a lookout.

3: **Embryo in development**
Female saltwater crocodiles lay around

50 eggs. While incubating, young
crocodiles form a toothed area on
their snout called an egg tooth, which
they use to help break open the shell.
After two to three months, the babies
are ready to hatch.

Sea Snakes

All snakes can swim, but sea snakes are so well-adapted to life underwater that most never leave their ocean home. Born in the water, sea snakes will spend their whole lives swimming, diving beneath the surface to hunt for prey and returning to the surface to breathe air. Although all sea snakes evolved from land snakes, only one group of sea snakes (sea kraits) still moves to solid ground to have their young. Most species have lost the rough scales on their underside, which means they cannot grip dry terrain. A true sea snake is not able to glide like a land snake.

Sea snakes have flat, paddle-like tails, small heads, and thin bodies, which enable them to cut through the water. Because sea snakes are cold-blooded reptiles and need to get their heat from the environment, they must stay in warm water. This means they are limited to tropical parts of the ocean, with many staying close to the coast. Other sea snakes are pelagic (living in the open ocean) and use ocean currents to help them move around.

Fresh water can be hard to come by in the ocean, but sea snakes need to drink. Some wait for it to rain, and drink from the layer of fresh water on the surface of the sea. Any salt they accidentally ingest is secreted from around their tongue and spat back into the water. Because sea snakes need warmer water and a reliable source of fresh water, they cannot live in the Atlantic—any routes into this ocean, such as around the Cape of Good Hope in South Africa, are too cold and have very little rain.

Sea snakes have a potent venom that is delivered through a bite and can be used either defensively or to catch their prey of fish and small octopuses. This venom is a neurotoxin, which causes muscles in the victim to stop working (paralysis) so the snake can eat without risking harm to itself. It is very rare for people to be bitten by sea snakes, and fatalities are almost unheard of.

Key to plate

1: **Turtle-headed sea snake**
Emydocephalus annulatus
Length: Up to 35 inches/
90 centimeters
This snake has venom that is quite weak, and it will often retreat rather than try to bite in defense. It feeds only on fish eggs.

2: **Yellow-bellied sea snake**
Hydrophis platurus
Length: Up to 35 inches/
90 centimeters
This snake is entirely pelagic, diving underwater to hunt. It can breathe through its skin, which helps it to stay underwater for longer.

3: **Yellow-lipped sea krait**
Laticauda colubrina
Length: Up to 5 feet/1.5 meters
Sea kraits such as this one are semiaquatic. They spend time on land to lay their eggs and to digest food, and only go to sea to hunt for their prey. Because of this, sea kraits are often found along coasts.

4: **Olive sea snake**
Aipysurus laevis
Length: Up to 6½ feet/2 meters
Like all snakes, the olive sea snake has to shed its skin, or molt, periodically. It does this by using the coral reef to snag the edges of its skin and peeling

it off slowly. Molting helps snakes to grow and rids them of parasites that attach themselves to their skin.

5: **Belcher's sea snake**
Hydrophis belcheri
Length: Up to 3 feet/1 meter
This sea snake is highly venomous but docile and rarely attacks humans. If it does, it doesn't always inject toxin, and its short teeth often won't pierce through a diver's wetsuit.

Habitat: Galápagos Islands

The Galápagos Islands are located on the equator, 600 miles/1,000 kilometers west of Ecuador. Rising from the depths of the Pacific Ocean 9,800 feet/3,000 meters below the surface, this chain of islands was formed by ancient volcanic activity, and there are still active volcanoes on some of the islands today.

Although they are located where the climate is usually hot, the Galápagos generally experience cool, drizzly weather. This is because the Humboldt Current—a 500-mile-/ 800-kilometer-wide strip of cold, nutrient-rich water—passes the Galápagos, not only cooling the air above it but also providing the nutrients needed for phytoplankton to bloom, which triggers hundreds of different food chains.

Both above and below the water, the islands are home to a range of species, many of which occur nowhere else on earth. This is known as endemism and is a common feature of island ecosystems, where species evolve in isolation, far from the mainland. One of the most famous examples of an endemic species from the Galápagos is that of the marine iguana—the only iguana in the world to swim in the sea. These reptiles graze on algae growing on rocks underwater and return to land to bask in the sun and warm themselves. They were documented by Charles Darwin in 1835 during his travels on board the HMS *Beagle* (he described them as "most disgusting, clumsy lizards") and were among the creatures that inspired him to develop his theory of evolution and write *On the Origin of Species*.

Around three thousand marine species, many of them endemic, live and feed in the Galápagos region. Because these populations are so vulnerable, the islands have been designated a marine protected area (MPA) by the government of Ecuador, covering around 51,000 square miles/130,000 square kilometers. By limiting fishing and protecting wildlife, the MPA aims to preserve the unique nature of this incredible corner of the world.

Key to plate

Galápagos coastline, Republic of Ecuador

1: Magnificent frigatebird
Fregata magnificens
Wingspan: Up to 8 feet/2.4 meters
These huge birds are known to peck at other seabirds to make them regurgitate their food so the frigatebirds can steal it for themselves.

2: Galápagos penguin
Spheniscus mendiculus
Length: Approx. 19 inches/ 49 centimeters
This small penguin can live in this tropical location only because of the cool waters of the Humboldt Current.

3: Marine iguana
Amblyrhynchus cristatus

Length: Up to 5 feet/1.5 meters
The only marine lizards in the world, these iguanas have blunt snouts that can scrape algae off underwater rocks.

4: Flightless cormorant
Phalacrocorax harrisi
Length: Up to 3 feet/1 meter
These birds evolved without any predators, so with no need to fly, they gradually lost the ability to do so. Humans later introduced cats and dogs to the islands, making the cormorants vulnerable to predation.

5: Sally lightfoot crab
Grapsus grapsus
Carapace width: Up to 3 inches/ 8 centimeters
These beautiful crabs live on the rocks just above the water and are very agile.

6: Bullseye pufferfish
Sphoeroides annulatus
Length: Approx. 7 inches/ 18 centimeters
This pufferfish's name comes from the circular markings on its back.

7: Scalloped hammerhead shark
Sphyrna lewini
Length: Up to 10 feet/3 meters
The iconic head of this shark gives it a wider field of vision.

8: King angelfish
Holacanthus passer
Length: Approx. 6 inches/ 15 centimeters
Males and females will pair for a whole breeding season, meeting to spawn every day.

Gallery 9

One Ocean

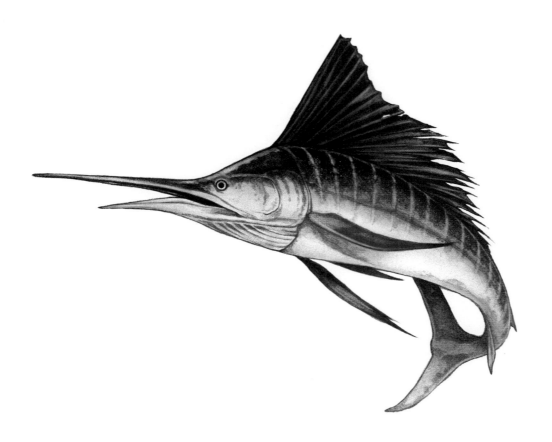

Habitat: Open Ocean

Humans and the Ocean

Habitat: Open Ocean

Move away from the coast and you will eventually reach the open ocean: a vast expanse of water where there is no land in sight. The animals found here have adapted to survive the challenges of an environment where food is scarce and the distances are enormous.

The open ocean, also known as the pelagic zone, extends from the water's surface to just above the seabed. Below 660 feet/200 meters there is little or no sunlight, so most creatures congregate in the upper waters, where sunlight enables phytoplankton to photosynthesize. As do all plants, phytoplankton need nutrients. In the ocean, these come from the land, carried by rivers and streams to the sea. In large parts of the open ocean these nutrients don't reach the surface, but where they do, they feed enormous blooms of phytoplankton, providing food for a huge variety of ocean creatures.

Smaller animals often form shoals that provide protection from predators through safety in numbers—predators are faced with a mass of moving fish, making it difficult to pick out any one. But when predators target a shoal, it can become a bait ball; the fish swim closer together, shifting and changing direction in a split second to respond to the movements of the hunters. Bait balls can attract a number of larger predators, each with their own approach to capturing a meal. Dolphins work together to push the ball of fish toward the surface, taking turns to dash in. Tuna and sharks rely on their speed, power, and agility to outswim individual fish, while bulk feeders such as whales lunge through the middle of the shoal, consuming hundreds of fish all at once. When the feeding frenzy has finished, the predators continue on their way, often leaving little more than scales drifting down into the deep.

The story of the open ocean doesn't end there, as ocean predators are not the only hunters in this realm. Humans often frequent these waters to catch many species of fish to feed people back on land. But overfishing is putting a strain on the sea's dwindling resources. We must recognize that there is only one ocean that supports all life on our planet.

Key to plate

Open waters, Pacific Ocean

1: **Blue flying fish**
Exocoetus volitans
Length: Approx. 8 inches/
20 centimeters
Flying fish use their winglike fins to glide above the water's surface. They can usually "fly" around 164 feet/ 50 meters, but on an updraft can travel up to 1,300 feet/400 meters!

2: **Mahi-mahi**
Coryphaena hippurus
Length: Approx. 3 feet/1 meter
Females lay between 100,000 and 1 million eggs at once, two to three times a year, meaning mahi-mahi are plentiful.

3: **Silky shark**
Carcharhinus falciformis
Length: Approx. 8 feet/2.5 meters
These sleek hunters are one of the most common open ocean sharks, found in warmer waters worldwide.

4: **Pacific herring**
Clupea pallasii
Length: Approx. 10 inches/
25 centimeters
This small fish is vital to numerous ocean food chains. Herring fishing also supports many communities along the Pacific coast of the United States.

5: **Indo-Pacific sailfish**
Istiophorus platypterus
Length: Approx. 9 feet/2.7 meters

Widely thought to be the fastest fish in the world, this species has been recorded at speeds of up to 68 miles/ 110 kilometers per hour.

6: **Yellowfin tuna**
Thunnus albacares
Length: Approx. 5 feet/1.5 meters
Yellowfin tuna swim in large schools, often with other animals, such as dolphins or other species of tuna.

7: **Pacific white-sided dolphin**
Lagenorhynchus obliquidens
Length: Approx. 7 feet/2 meters
White-sided dolphins often travel in super pods, which are groups of up to 100 individuals.

Humans and the Ocean

The ocean is one of humanity's greatest resources. Eight-thousand-year-old archaeological evidence showing the remains of primitive dugout canoes suggests that humans have had a relationship with the ocean for millennia. Over the years, we have reaped the benefits of this resource, using it for food, travel, medicine, tourism, and more recently, as a source of renewable energy. Due to its immense size, it was once thought that the ocean was inexhaustible, but we now know this is not the case.

With a growing population, our dependence on the ocean has never been greater. Our sometimes excessive consumption of resources has led to environmental issues that impact humanity as well as wildlife around the world. Overfishing and pollution from plastics, oil, and greenhouse gases have led to parts of the ocean being unable to support the life they once did. But this can change.

The ocean is resilient and can recover if given time. Scientific studies have shown that damage to the environment can be reversed if protective measures are put in place. Marine scientists and engineers have more knowledge and technology at their disposal than ever before, which have led to initiatives such as wind farms that provide sources of green energy; the establishment of protected marine habitats that ensure the survival of endangered species; more sustainable fishing practices; and improved ways of living that can reduce our global carbon footprint. People are increasingly aware of the problems facing our planet and are seeking out ways to help. Whether by making small changes to our everyday lives or by actively spreading the message of conservation, together, we can make a difference for a positive future.

Key to plate

1: **Offshore wind farm**
Wind farms help to produce clean, renewable energy. The wind's share of US electricity generation increased from 7.4% in 2019 to 8.8% in 2020.

2: **Agricultural runoff**
Pesticides used on crops can wash into rivers and flow into oceans, causing harm to many marine animals and triggering dangerous algal blooms (see page 10).

3: **Large fishing boat**
Large ships can spend weeks at sea, catching thousands of tons of fish.

4: **Sustainable fish farms**
Sustainable fish farms are sensitive to the local environment and avoid using harmful chemicals. They provide ethically raised, healthy food for people without threatening fish populations in their natural ecosystem.

5: **Ecotourism**
Ecotourism encourages support for local communities and marine habitats while promoting conservation and preservation.

6: **Marine protected area (MPA)**
Only around 4 percent of the world's ocean is protected, but studies have proven these areas are effective in allowing fish populations to recover. In the Philippines, for example, numbers of surgeonfish and jackfish have tripled in one protected area since it was established almost two decades ago.

7: **Coral bleaching**
Microscopic algae give color and nutrients to coral reefs. But when the ocean's temperature rises or its chemical composition is altered, the algae cannot survive. The coral then loses its food source and color and appears bleached (see page 22).

Library

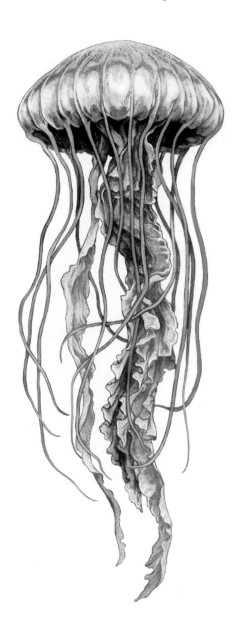

Index

Curators

Loveday Trinick is a marine biologist working as a Schools Officer for the Ocean Conservation Trust. Based at the National Marine Aquarium in Plymouth, she teaches children of all ages about the ocean and why it is important to all of us. Loveday Trinick loves seeing kids inspired by animals and creating connections to the marine environment. She believes this is the best way to help conserve the ocean for future generations.

Teagan White is an artist and illustrator living in the Pacific Northwest. They use depictions of flora and fauna to celebrate the intricate beauty of the natural world and to highlight the fraught relationship between humans and the rest of nature. Teagan White is currently a member of the University of Washington's Coastal Observation and Seabird Survey Team (COASST) and Oregon Shores' CoastWatch—two citizen science projects dedicated to monitoring ecosystem health and public land use, by collecting baseline data to help assess patterns of seabird mortality due to natural and human-induced events.

To Learn More

Census of Marine Life
This website is the result of a global, decade-long initiative by more than 2,700 scientists. Fully comprehensive, the database catalogues over 30 million records that feature updates on new species, marine conservation, habitat monitoring, and recent discoveries.
http://www.coml.org/index.html

Marine Conservation Society
This society's website has great ideas for working toward a more sustainable and environmentally friendly planet.
https://www.mcsuk.org

National Geographic
Test your knowledge with National Geographic's ocean quizzes and learn more through interactive games.
https://www.nationalgeographic.com

National Marine Aquarium
The UK's largest aquarium has developed a learning program in conjunction with the Ocean Conservation Trust and national curriculum guidelines.
https://www.national-aquarium.co.uk

National Oceanic and Atmospheric Administration (NOAA)
This US government agency has an extensive range of resources, perfect for students who want to explore climate change, marine life, pollution, and much more.
https://www.noaa.gov

The Ocean Conservation Trust
With a whole host of online projects to take part in, this organization runs initiatives that encourage people to think about the ocean via positive experiences and connections.
https://oceanconservationtrust.org

Oceana's Marine Life Encyclopedia
Discover each ocean creature in more detail in the fully comprehensive Marine Life Encyclopedia.
https://oceana.org/marine-life

Sea Trust
This nonprofit organization regularly updates their website with wildlife sightings around the UK.
https://seatrust.org.uk

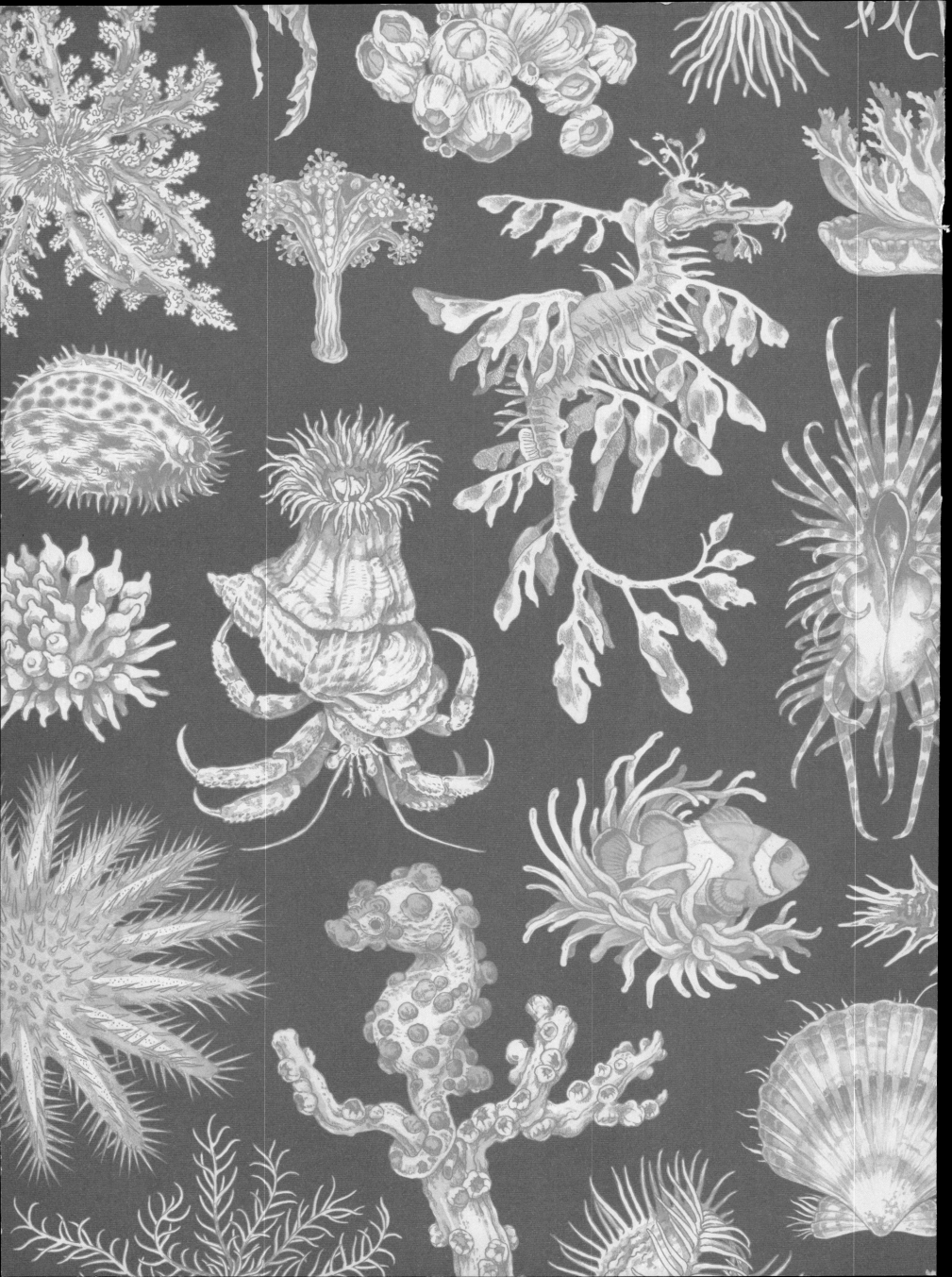